Social
Policy
AN INTRODUCTION

RICHARD M. TITMUSS

Social
Policy

AN INTRODUCTION

Edited by
Brian Abel-Smith and Kay Titmuss

London
GEORGE ALLEN & UNWIN LTD
RUSKIN HOUSE   MUSEUM STREET

ISBN 0 04 361018 8 Paperback

Printed in Great Britain
in 12-point Fournier type
by William Clowes & Sons, Limited
London, Beccles and Colchester

CONTENTS

INTRODUCTION

Richard Titmuss died on 6 April 1973. This book is an edited version of a course of introductory lectures which he gave at the London School of Economics for many years. He delivered these lectures for the last time during the three months preceding his death.

Although the series was given on many occasions, each year the lectures were revised. New material was incorporated and earlier material was discarded. Occasionally a whole lecture would be completely redesigned and rewritten. This book is an edited version of his notes. No recordings were made of the lectures as actually delivered. Most of what he said was drawn from a carefully prepared verbatim script but there were occasional passages when the script slipped into note form – usually a prompt for one of his vivid illustrations. The general sense of these passages could be ascertained without difficulty and a paragraph has been inserted to give the drift of what he would have said. Often supporting press cuttings were to be found in the same file as his lecture notes which could be used in text or footnotes as seemed appropriate.

Editing has been kept to the minimum. No one would be so presumptuous as to imagine that they could improve upon Titmuss' musical prose. What has been done is to remove the first person singular which we thought would irritate when presented in book form. Indeed, this was his usual practice when editing his own lectures for publication. In the process several 'I think's' have been deleted and this has made some passages read in a more didactic way than when delivered as a lecture. Also deleted are occasional passages and references, particularly in the first lecture, that were parochial. For example, he explained how this series of lectures related to other teaching at the LSE and occasionally mentioned colleagues and LSE institutions which would mean nothing to the general reader.

The arrangement into chapters does not follow the lectures in every case. The opportunity has been taken to make a clearer division by subject. Titmuss often used to complain about the difficulty of dealing with a subject in a lecture of exactly fifty minutes. In practice, he seldom followed his own division of his material: he would take longer than he had intended in presenting an example or answering a question. The lectures published as Chapters 7 and 10 were discarded from the eight lectures he delivered or planned to deliver in 1973.

Titmuss' books are widely read in the United States and elsewhere. Special care has therefore been taken to ensure that British institutions are broadly intelligible to North American and other students of social policy.

It should perhaps be emphasised that these were introductory lectures. It is for this reason that Titmuss takes time to explain the content of books which will be well known to those who are familiar with the field. While there is thus more straightforward quotation, summarisation and explanation than in most of Titmuss' work, there are nevertheless passages which we found as penetrating and thought-provoking as any of his other works.

While we have been able to amend, delete and re-arrange, we cannot add to the text. Indeed, it would be wrong to try to do so. If Titmuss had asked us what the lectures needed if he had been preparing them for publication himself, we would have asked him to say more about the models of social policy described at the end of Chapter 2, to give a stronger underlying unity to the book. There is at present an unevenness of treatment. Much is said about Model A, the *Residual Welfare Model*, but there is little direct discussion of the other two models. To this extent, the book is somewhat unfinished.

Incorporated as a postscript is a passage which Titmuss actually used to introduce the first of his lectures in 1973 and explain why he was delivering his lecture series in the second rather than the first term of the academic year as originally scheduled. It would have given the wrong impression of the book to have included it at the start. This was the last piece of any length that Titmuss wrote. It is included here partly we confess, for sentimental reasons and partly because it conveys something personal about the man – more than in any of his work so far published. Moreover, it provides an encouraging ending. It shows that, in his last few months, Titmuss felt that his work and the work of many others (as he would insist on us adding) was not entirely in vain. The British National Health Service, as he experienced it, was practising the moral principles in which he believed so passionately.

We wish to thank Mrs Harriet Bretherton for finding and checking the references. We owe a great debt to Ann and Howard Glennerster, Ida Merriam, Ann and Robin Oakley, David Piachaud and Garth Plowman, who all read the book carefully before it went to the press and contributed many valuable comments which we have used in our final revision. For any errors in the editing which remain we must take responsibility. We have tried to be as conscientious as Richard himself always was before he allowed anything he wrote to appear in print.

Brian Abel-Smith
Kay C. Titmuss

December 1973

1

The International Perspective

One belief, more than any others, is responsible for
the slaughter of individuals on the altars of the great
historical ideals – justice or progress or the
happiness of future generations, or the sacred mission
or emancipation of a nation or race or class, or even
liberty itself, which demands the sacrifice of
individuals for the freedom of society. This is the
belief that somewhere, in the past or in the future, in
divine revelation or in the mind of an individual
thinker, in the pronouncements of history or science, or in
the simple heart of an uncorrupted good man, there is
a final solution. This ancient faith rests on the
conviction that all the positive values in which men
have believed must, in the end, be compatible, and
perhaps even entail one another.[1]

Not all good things are compatible, still less are all the ideals
of mankind. This is as true in the realm of social policy as in
other areas of human life. What is social policy? Can a distinction be made between social policy and economic policy?

We live in an age of 'the great simplifiers' brought into
being, in part, by the mass consumption society. The simplifiers are dominated by the mass media of the press and particularly of television. They must see everything in terms of
black versus white and present polarised conflict as enter-

[1] Berlin, I., *Four Essays on Liberty*, Oxford University Press, Oxford, 1969, p. 167.

tainment – the universalists versus the selectivists, the spoon-fed versus the independent, or individual choice versus the rationing state.

Many reasons can be given for the simplification, trivialisation and denigration of political and moral issues. How far do editors lose control of their star reporters after they have built them up? How far do the promotion and rewards of journalists (no longer anonymous) depend more than ever on the presentation of scandal and violence – for example student violence.[1] How far does audience-rating encourage the presentation of serious issues as trivial entertainment? How far does the fear of loss of advertising revenue limit criticism of the private market? Is this why scandal about Government is so much more newsworthy than scandal about the private sector?

It is fashionable to believe that all power and authority and all politicians are evil. Just as academic freedom can justify anything (what Tawney once called 'creating a darkness and calling it research'), and clinical freedom justifies private practice and profit-making hospitals in the USA, so the freedom of the press can justify mass entertainment, the commercial-isation of sex and the commercialisation of privacy. As these unlimited freedoms become more pervasive, society – and particularly at this point in history American society – becomes harder and harder to govern. It is not widely known that during the first six months of 1971 more people were murdered in New York alone than all the American soldiers killed in Vietnam during the same six months. Violence and theft have reached such a scale that public assistance officers are armed. Even in the School of Social Work, New York University, all

---

[1] 'There has never been a time when some students have not occasionally been riotous. What is new is the preoccupation of the news media with violence. The news value of violence is an open invitation to those who wish to air their views or grievances to resort to violence for the purpose, and it is too much to expect that students should be wholly immune from this temptation. I have heard of a case in which student violence towards a controversial figure was actively encouraged and stage-managed by cameramen. Students who behave like this are, however, a small minority and the prominence given to them results in a student image which is grotesquely distorted.' Sir Edward Hale, letter to *The Times*, 21 December 1972.

typewriters, adding machines, tape recorders and other equipment are chained and bolted to the floor.

Poor people in blighted ghetto areas of the USA are no longer able to purchase insurance for their homes and contents against the risks of fire, burglary, theft and vandalism. The insurance industry, with assets totalling over $208 billion, have now declared the inner core, the blighted centres of cities, as uninsurable risks. All the inhabitants, therefore, black and white, are 'bad risks', uninsurable against the risks of violence, vandalism, riots, fire and death. In a recent Report[1] to the President, the main recommendation (so far not implemented) was that Government must come to the rescue; Government must take over the 'bad risks' of the richest society the world has ever known. This, in effect, was a social policy directive – and also an example of the problem of defining the boundaries of social policy in theory and practice.

There are lessons in all this, lessons to be learnt from history, when we try to understand the issues of freedom and licence, law and discretion, justice and punishment, poverty and stigma, equity and equality. Where does social policy begin, and where does it end? How is it possible to describe its scope, meaning, content, formation, execution, principles and theory?

At best it is clear that the study of social policy cannot be isolated from the study of society as a whole in all its varied social, economic and political aspects. An essential background for the study of social policy is a knowledge of population changes, past and present and predicted for the future; the family as an institution and the position of women; social stratification and the concepts of class, caste, status and mobility, social change and the effects of industrialisation, urbanisation and social conditions; the political structure; the work ethic and the sociology of industrial relations; minority groups and racial prejudice; social control, conformity,

---

[1] *Meeting the Insurance Crisis of our Cities.* A Report by the President's Advisory Panel, US Government Printing Office, Washington DC, 1968.

deviance and the uses of sociology to maintain the political status quo.

Policy, any policy, to be effective must choose an objective and must face dilemmas of choice. But to understand policy, to distinguish between ends (what we want or think we want) and means (how we get there), we have to see it in the context of a particular set of circumstances, a given society and culture, and a more or less specified period of historical time. In other words, social policy cannot be discussed or even conceptualised in a social vacuum – unlike the Robinson Crusoe idea of Economic Man.

This book is largely about policies in British society: most of the materials and illustrations are derived from British experience but comparative materials are also used from other countries. The British are not alone or in any sense unique in devising systems of 'welfare'. There is now a very extensive international literature relating to systems of welfare in developed and developing countries.

During the last ten years over one hundred books have been published in the United States alone on such subjects as 'poverty', 'deprivation' and 'welfare rights' – most of them at a high level of simplification. Quite a lot of money has been made in writing about poverty. It is financially more rewarding than working as public servants to improve services for poor people. It is therefore not surprising that poor people in Chicago and New York, and particularly black poor people, have sought to bring to an end research on poverty, environmental pollution, 'Headstart' programmes, community participation evaluations, and so forth. 'You', they pointedly say, 'have got a lot of Ph.D.s and books out of us. What have we got?' This is quite a sensible consumer question about the Ph.D. supermarket.

The more one attempts to study the international literature about different national social policy institutions, the more one becomes aware of the diversity and complexity. The more one understands this complexity, the more difficult does it become to generalise (to simplify pragmatically) about the different roles that social services are supposed to play – and do actually play – in different countries.

Soviet Russia, for example, has fashioned a model of social welfare which is based, in large measure, on the principles of work-performance, achievement and meritocratic selection. Wage and salary differentials between the top and bottom of the Russian Civil Service (which includes few black Russians from the East and the South because no Muslims from Central Asia and the Caucasus are allowed to become members of the Communist Party) are larger than wage-salary differentials in the British Civil Service. The social security system tends to legitimate – and even enhance – these differentials. This is especially so for working-class women who do much of the unskilled, dirty work – like street cleaning and lavatory attendance – in the Soviet Union. Lenin's belief that Communism would liberate women has not yet been fulfilled. In the Russian system of public assistance, as in Germany and France, grandchildren and grandparents are responsible for relatives. Their financial resources are assessed to see whether they can be expected to support the claimant. In Britain only the resources 'for husband and wife in the same household, together with those of any dependent children living with them, are each added and treated as the husband's'.[1]

Other Soviet social services – like the mental health services – are, in part, social control mechanisms (they perform a police function) in respect of dissenters, non-conformers, deviants and under-achievers. In part, they also function to sustain and glorify the work ethic (as do the boarding schools in Russia which are preoccupied with character-building and the value of hard physical labour).

When, however, all social services expenditures are aggregated and expressed as a percentage of personal money income for Russia and the United Kingdom, Professor Wiles and Mr Markowski argue that the Russian expenditures were in the

[1] DHSS, *Supplementary Benefits Handbook*, HMSO, London, November 1972, p. 8.

late 1950s more redistributive than in the UK.[1] What is not known, however (and that is the trouble with Professor Wiles' statistics), is whether redistribution favours the higher or lower income groups. The effects of the social security system – taken alone – do indicate that the higher income groups receive proportionately higher rewards. In short, the objectives and the results are based on work performance and achieved work earnings.

In the area of social security, West Germany has a not dissimilar model for its pension programme from that operating in the Soviet Union. Again it is fundamentally based on work rewards, productivity, achievement and merit. There is virtually no element of redistribution built into the system. Its model, geared to dynamism, is based on the private insurance market.

Underpinning and supporting this work-reward system is the presence of $2\frac{1}{4}$ million guest workers, or '*Gastarbeiters*', medically examined by German doctors in the country of origin, and recruited from Turkey, Greece, North Africa, Southern Italy, Yugoslavia, Spain and Portugal. The great majority of these two million or so workers do not have their families with them; about 75 per cent are men, and nearly all are engaged in the unskilled dirty, menial and domestic tasks of the modern economy. They are all on one-year permits to one employer, renewable on good conduct and (subject to fluctuations in the employment situation) by the authority of that employer.

In the event of serious illness, disability, injury, mental breakdown, alcoholism, homelessness, drug addiction or of offences against the civil or criminal codes these workers are put on trains or planes and sent home. Similarly, single women workers who become pregnant or produce illegitimate children are returned to their families. They have no voting rights, no welfare rights, no rights to public assistance which

---

[1] Wiles, P. J. D. and Markowski, S., 'Income Distribution under Communism and Capitalism', in *Soviet Studies*, Nos. 3 and 4, 1971.

in Germany, as in all the Common Market countries as well as Scandinavia, is a municipal responsibility with rights varying between different local authorities – as it was in Britain before the 1930s. Even if they were eligible, the levels of social assistance (or social aid) from the municipal authorities are so low (as they are in the Irish Republic) that the system acts as a deterrent.

The situation of the million or so Irish immigrants in Britain (including their wives and large families) is different. Levels of Supplementary Benefits and Allowances for these families plus Family Allowances are far higher than earnings for unskilled workers in the Irish Republic and thus act as a magnet for poor Irish families dependent either on parish relief or charity from the Church (especially for the category known as 'fallen women'). Irish immigrants, temporary, pseudo-temporary and permanent, represent one of the major factors in the rising number of claimants and recipients of Supplementary Allowances in recent years and thus complicate any estimates of the number of adults and children 'in poverty' or on the margins of poverty in Britain.

We have, thus, a situation in which the Irish Republic, partly because of a lack of any national organised system of public assistance, exports a proportion of its public assistance – or potential public assistance – cases to Britain. West Germany, for very different reasons and with a far higher standard of living than Eire, also exports a major part of its public assistance problem – but to much poorer countries. And it is not simply a question of the provision of means-tested cash assistance for people with social handicaps, the newly disabled and chronic sick, ex-prisoners and their families, alcoholics, deserted wives, unmarried mothers and so forth. Many of these people (among the 'under-class' as certain American sociologists would describe them) also need child care and welfare services, provision for homelessness, social work support and a more generous input of educational provision.

It is indeed arguable that a country which, at one and the

same time, can maintain a flexible pool of some two million unskilled workers and relatively smaller public assistance and welfare programmes, is economically in a better position to sustain a higher rate of economic growth. Nor is it likely to lead to the same degree to pressures from unskilled temporary workers to narrow wage differentials through trade union action. Consequently, the dangers of inflation in the economy become less.

In all the debates in recent years about international differences in the rate of growth of gross national product, particularly among the Common Market countries, economists have generally neglected these issues. This is partly because economists make a sharp distinction, at least in theory, between what constitutes economic policy and what constitutes social policy. It can also, of course, be said that many writers on social policy – or the social services – suffer from the same tendency to compartmentalise their subjects. Few social services textbooks, for example, have much to say about the social costs of unemployment, about regional economic policies (though such policies may be critically important in reducing social and educational inequalities between regions) or about the examples given above on the inter-connections between the unskilled market in labour and the role of public assistance programmes. One major exception, among economists and social policy writers, is Professor Kenneth Boulding. Both in *Principles of Economic Policy*[1] and in an article, 'The Boundaries of Social Policy',[2] he attempted to draw together and analyse comprehensively both the social and the economic components of policy and its application in practice.[3]

These illustrations from the Soviet Union, Ireland and West Germany are intended simply to show the difficulties of

[1] Boulding, K. E., *Principles of Economic Policy*, Staples, London, 1968.

[2] Boulding, K. E., 'The Boundaries of Social Policy', *Social Work*, Vol. 12, No. 1, January 1967.

[3] See Titmuss, R. M., *Commitment to Welfare*, Allen & Unwin, London, 1968, Ch. 1, for a discussion of his contribution to the debate on the definition of social policy.

generalising in any universal sense about social policy and the many conflicting and different roles that such policies (or particular programmes) play in different societies. Many more examples could be given and questions asked about the wider implications of social programmes. What are the objectives of recent changes in the family allowance system in Israel which discriminate against Arabs and against those Jews who have not served in the Israeli armed forces?[1] What are the objectives of pension arrangements in France which provide higher old-age pensions for those who have had three or more children? Can public assistance programmes in the United States and other countries be regarded as elements of social policy when they compel unmarried mothers and deserted wives with children over the age of three to register for work and to accept *any* work offered to them by the Department of Labour? Should they not, on another view, be classified as labour control mechanisms and as part of a work-ethic value system not dissimilar from the provisions of the 1834 Poor Law (Amendment) Act in England? Finally, and by way of contrast, can one regard the Tanzanian Arusha Declaration of 1967, which emphasised the values of self-reliance, work and collective village development, as representing a social or an economic policy for that country?[2]

The United Nations has brought together much of this world-wide literature under such labels as 'Social Welfare Programmes', 'The World Social Situation', 'The Administration of Social Services', 'Social Planning and Social Development'. The word 'social' (not to be confused with sociological) is one word which all these titles have in common. This suggests that the central political issues of ends and means for the governments of all countries, rich and poor, cannot be thought of wholly in economic terms.

'Social policy' must therefore be analysed in a broad political

---

[1] Higher allowances are provided for the families of ex-Servicemen.

[2] Nyerere, J. K., *Ujamaa: essays on socialism*, Oxford University Press, Dar es Salaam, 1968.

and geographical framework. The perspective gained from comparative studies helps in the understanding of the social policies of one's own country. There is now a larger and increasing body of knowledge about social policy and welfare programmes in many different countries which cannot be ignored. When we study welfare systems in other countries, we see that they reflect the dominant cultural and political characteristics of their societies. But we have, nevertheless, to recognise that they are all concerned fundamentally with certain common human needs and problems.

2

What is Social Policy?

In the chapters that follow we look first at the term 'social policy' and ask a good many questions about it. In doing so, we shall inevitably have to consider various definitions of associated concepts and categorised labels – social administration, social services, social welfare, social security, welfare states and so forth. We will have to ask ourselves why we should study social policy at all or, for that matter, society's response as it identifies or fails to identify social needs and problems. Are we concerned with principles and objectives about certain areas of social life and organisation – or with social engineering: with methods and techniques of action, management, organisation and the application of games theory?

Whatever the answer we arrive at, we cannot fail to become heavily involved in the issues of moral and political values. Indeed, political propaganda frequently masquerades under social policy labels.

What do we mean by social policy? Connected with this is the equally important question: whose social policy? For our purposes the word 'policy' can be taken to refer to the principles that govern action directed towards given ends. The concept denotes action about means as well as ends and it, therefore, implies change: changing situations, systems, practices, behaviour. And here we should note that the concept of policy is only meaningful if we (society, a group, or an

organisation) believe we can affect change in some form or
another. We do not have policies about the weather because,
as yet, we are powerless to do anything about the weather. But
we do have policies (or we can have policies) about illegitimate children because we think we have some power to affect
their lives – for better or worse depending on whether you are
the policy-maker or the illegitimate child.

The word 'policy' is used here in an action-oriented and
problem-oriented sense. The collective 'we' is used to refer to
the actions of government in expressing the 'general will' of
the people – whether of Britain, Nigeria or China. The meaning
and validity of a concept of the 'general will' is, of course,
hotly debated.

The greatest semantic difficulty arises, inevitably, with the
word 'social'. Nor is it made any easier today by the fact that
so many disciplines, professions and groups claim it as a
Christian name and, indeed, flourish it about as something
distinctly different. We have, for example, social geography,
social planning, social psychology, social psychiatry, social
administration, social work, social law, social linguistics,
social history, social medicine, social pathology, and so on.
Even the Bank of America created in January 1972 a new post
of executive vice-president in charge of social policy! Why not
social theology? Is it really necessary to drive home so pon-
derously the fact that all these subjects and groups are concerned in some way with man in society – and particularly
with the non-economic factors in human relations? Are they
not all, in short, emphasising that man is a social being; that
he is not solely Economic Man; and that society cannot be
thought of in terms of mechanistic-organic models or physio-
logical models? It may well be that much of the current fashion
for 'social' is a reaction against the sillier models of man in
society constructed in the past by economists, political philosophers, experimental psychologists and sociologists.

Take, for example, the attempts of the Victorian economists
to establish a competitive, self-regulating total market

economy, or Radcliffe-Brown's doctrine (as one of the 'fathers' of modern anthropology) that the organic nature of society is a fact. Such a doctrine implies that integration and solidarity must be 'natural' attributes of all social systems. 'Social structures', he wrote, 'are just as real as are individual organisms. A complex organism is a collection of living cells and interstitial fluids arranged in a certain structure. . . .'[1]

This is what another anthropologist, a *social* anthropologist, Edmund Leach, had to say about this doctrine: 'If you feel certain, on *a priori* grounds, that all forms of social stress must produce a reaction which will tend to restore or even reinforce the solidarity (i.e. organic health) of society then you will quickly persuade yourself that war is peace and conflict harmony.'[2]

You might argue, if social stresses correct themselves automatically (on the analogy of the self-regulating market economy), then there is no place for an unpredictable concept like social policy.

But it can, of course, be argued that social policy (or, to be more precise, a system of social welfare) is simply part of the self-regulatory mechanisms built into a 'natural' social system. This would mean that the history of the development of the social services in Britain since the beginning of the twentieth century was, in a sense, predetermined; that it was bound to happen because of a 'natural' tendency in the social system toward equilibrium and order. Some part of the theory of Talcott Parsons sustains this equilibrium-order concept.[3] Fundamentally, it is a conservative ideology akin to the philosophy that 'All is for the best in this best of all possible worlds,' – or akin, to take another analogy, to neo-classical economic theory with its conception of the best possible self-regulating supply and demand private market (largely, as the

[1] Radcliffe-Brown, A. R., *Structure and Function in Primitive Society*, Cohen & West, London, 1952, p. 190.

[2] Leach, E., 'Models', *New Society*, 14 May 1964.

[3] See, for example, Talcott Parsons, *The Structure of Social Action*, Allen & Unwin, London, 1949; and *The Social System*, Routledge & Kegan Paul, London, 1964.

Women's Liberation Movement has pointed out, a private market for men).

All this is a rather roundabout way of saying that these mechanistic theories of orderly man and society consign a minor subsidiary role to social policy; indeed, not a 'policy' role at all; a role similar to that assigned to the State in nine-teenth-century Britain by Lassalle when he wrote about 'the Night Watchman State' (the 'Law and Order State' in the language of the 1970s). Only in a very restricted and contra-dictory sense could it be said that Night Watchmen have *policies* – unless it can be argued that to watch and keep order and not to act and change is a policy.

At the other end of the spectrum of values is the rejection of the notion of a mechanistic or residual role for social policy. Social policy can be seen as a positive instrument of change; as an unpredictable, incalculable part of the whole political process.

We must not, however, jump to the conclusion that social policy as conceived in this or any other way is necessarily beneficent or welfare-oriented in the sense of providing more welfare and more benefits for the poor, the so-called working-classes, old-age pensioners, women, deprived children and other categories in the catalogue of social poverty. A redistri-butive social policy can redistribute command over material and non-material resources from the poor to the rich; from one ethnic group to another ethnic group; from working life to old age within income groups and social classes – as, for ex-ample, in middle-class pension schemes – and in other ways.

There are social policies in South Africa today which many people would not regard as being beneficent or welfare-oriented. There are social insurance programmes in some Latin American countries, Brazil in particular, which function as concealed multipliers of inequality – they transfer resources from the poor to the rich. Hitler developed social policies in Nazi Germany – they were in fact called social policies – con-cerning the mentally ill and retarded, the Jews and other ethnic groups. World public opinion condemned these instruments of social policy which had as their ultimate ends the use of human beings for medical research, sterilisation and the gas chamber.

When we use the term 'social policy' we must not, therefore, automatically react by investing it with a halo of altruism, concern for others, concern about equality and so on. Nor must we unthinkingly conclude that because Britain – or any other country – has a social policy or has developed social services, that they actually operate in practice to further the ends of progressive redistribution, equality and social altruism. What is 'welfare' for some groups may be 'illfare' for others.

And, lastly, in guarding against the value implications of the term 'social policy', I should point out that it does not imply allegiance to any political party or ideology. We all have our values and our prejudices; we all have our rights and duties as citizens, and our rights and duties as teachers and students. At the very least, we have a responsibility for making our values clear; and we have a special duty to do so when we are discussing such a subject as social policy which, quite clearly, has no meaning at all if it is considered to be neutral in terms of values. Or as Nye Bevan, the architect of the British National Health Service, was so fond of saying: 'This is my truth, now tell me yours.'[1]

Gunnar Myrdal has had much to say in his writings on economic and social policy about the dangers of deceiving ourselves and others about our values and biases. He has criticised sociologists and anthropologists for believing in the possibility of a value-free approach in their studies of social organisation.[2]

[1] 'Life with Nye', Jenny Lee, *The Observer* Colour Supplement, 10 December 1972.
[2] He did so first in his book *An American Dilemma: the Negro problem and modern democracy*, Harper & Row, London, 1962, and more recently in *The Challenge of World Poverty*, Allen Lane, London, 1970 (see Ch. 1, 'Cleansing the Approach from Biases').

Hume once said that the true sceptic should be as diffident of his philosophical doubts as of his philosophical convictions. Can we then say that a true believer should be as diffident of his philosophical convictions as of his philosophical doubts – so a true sceptic and a true believer would be one and the same? Is such a paragon possible? Can a man temper his doubts with assertion, and his assertions with doubt, and yet act in pursuit of certain social policy goals? Is this what in the ordinary life of decision-making some people call wisdom – the power to be both critical and practical, both speculative and pragmatic?[1]

To return, however, to this tiresome business of defining social policy. Let us consider what some other writers have said on the subject. At one extreme, we can find the most comprehensive definition in the statement by Professor Macbeath in his 1957 Hobhouse Lecture: 'Social policies are concerned with the right ordering of the network of relationships between men and women who live together in societies, or with the principles which should govern the activities of individuals and groups so far as they affect the lives and interests of other people.'[2]

It would be difficult to be more sweeping than that. It could easily be read as a grand definition of the scope of sociology; indeed, a definition that includes economics and all the social science disciplines. However, one should point out that it was Professor Macbeath's purpose to state the central issue in social policy – or any policy determined by Government to intervene in the life of the community. As he saw it, the central issue was between the self-regarding (egotistical) activities of man and the other-regarding (altruistic) activities. Professor Ginsberg took much the same position. Arguing that some forms of social policy are based on the notion of moral progress, he then used criteria of moral progress which are to be

---

[1] See Corbett, P., *Ideologies*, Hutchinson, London, 1965, p. 209.

[2] Macbeath G., 'Can Social Policies be Rationally Tested?', Hobhouse Memorial Trust lecture, Oxford University Press, 1957, p. 1.

found 'in the growing power of altruism over egoism'[1] brought about by a fusion of intelligence and concern for social justice and equality. *The Gift Relationship* was an attempt to provide a concrete illustration of this philosophical view from an international study of blood donor systems.[2]

At the other extreme, let us take Professor Hagenbuch's definition of social policy. 'Stated in general terms,' he said, 'the mainspring of social policy may be said to be the desire to ensure every member of the community certain minimum standards and certain opportunities.'[3] This I think is typical of many definitions offered by other writers in a large number of Western countries. It is similar also to the views expressed by the United Nations in a series of studies and reports in recent years: for example, in the *Report on the Organization and Administration of Social Services*[4] published in 1962.

These and similar definitions, whether one views them as limited or broad, all contain three objectives – and, of course, value judgements. First, they aim to be beneficent – policy is directed to provide welfare for citizens. Second, they include economic as well as non-economic objectives; for example, minimum wages, minimum standards of income maintenance and so on. Thirdly, they involve some measure of progressive redistribution in command-over-resources from rich to poor.

Dissenting somewhat from these views is Professor Lafitte of Birmingham – the only professor in Britain with the title 'Social Policy'. He sees social policy as being more concerned with the communal environment – with the provision of social amenity (urban renewal and national parks, for example, and measures against pollution, noise, etc.) which the individual cannot purchase in the market as a lone individual. He puts less emphasis on individual transfer payments (like pensions) and

---

[1] Ginsberg, M., *The Idea of Progress: a revaluation*, Methuen, London, 1953, p. 24.
[2] Titmuss, R. M., *The Gift Relationship*, Allen & Unwin, London, 1971.
[3] Hagenbuch, W., *Social Economics*, Nisbet, Welwyn, 1958, p. 205.
[4] *Report on the Organization and Administration of Social Services*, Report by Group of Experts to UN Secretary General (ST/SOA/44 and E/CN.5/360/Rev. 1), 1962.

argues that 'in the main social policy is an attempt to steer the life of society along channels it would not follow if left to itself'.[1] This is in some senses a more limited definition – but it does imply a substantial interventionist role by Government in the provision of a wide range of community facilities and safeguards.

Professor Marshall is more practical and down-to-earth: '"Social Policy" is not a technical term with an exact meaning ... it is taken to refer to the policy of governments with regard to action having a direct impact on the welfare of the citizens, by providing them with services or income. The central core consists, therefore, of social insurance, public (or national) assistance, the health and welfare services, housing policy.'[2]

Again, social policy is seen to be beneficent, redistributive and concerned with economic as well as non-economic objectives. Like many of the other definitions, social policy (as with economic policy) is all about 'what is and what might be'. It is thus involved in choices in the ordering of social change.

As an aid to our inquiries, it is helpful to examine three contrasting models or functions of social policy. The purpose of model-building is not to admire the architecture of the building, but to help us to see some order in all the disorder and confusion of facts, systems and choices concerning certain areas of our economic and social life. Tentatively, the three models can be described as follows:

MODEL A *The Residual Welfare Model of Social Policy*

This formulation is based on the premise that there are two 'natural' (or socially given) channels through which an individual's needs are properly met; the private market and the family. Only when these break down should social welfare

[1] Lafitte, F., *Social Policy in a Free Society*, Birmingham University Press, 1962, p. 9.
[2] Marshall, T. H., *Social Policy*, Hutchinson, London, 1965, p. 7.

institutions come into play and then only temporarily. As Professor Peacock puts it: 'The true object of the Welfare State is to teach people how to do without it.'[1] The theoretical basis of this model can be traced back to the early days of the English Poor Law, and finds support in organic-mechanistic-biological constructs of society advanced by sociologists like Spencer and Radcliffe-Brown, and economists like Friedman, Hayek and the founders and followers of the Institute of Economic Affairs in London.

MODEL B *The Industrial Achievement-Performance Model of Social Policy*

This incorporates a significant role for social welfare institutions as adjuncts of the economy. It holds that social needs should be met on the basis of merit, work performance and productivity. It is derived from various economic and psychological theories concerned with incentives, effort and reward, and the formation of class and group loyalties. It has been described as the 'Handmaiden Model'.

MODEL C *The Institutional Redistributive Model of Social Policy*

This model sees social welfare as a major integrated institution in society, providing universalist services outside the market on the principle of need. It is in part based on theories about the multiple effects of social change and the economic system, and in part on the principle of social equality. It is basically a model incorporating systems of redistribution in command-over-resources-through-time.

These three models are, of course, only very broad approximations to the theories and ideas of economists, philosophers, political scientists and sociologists. Many variants could be developed of a more sophisticated kind. However, these

---

[1] Peacock, A., *The Welfare Society*, Liberal Publication Department, London, 1960, p. 11.

approximations do serve to indicate the major differences – the ends of the value spectrum – in the views held about the means and ends of social policy. All three models involve consideration of the work ethic and the institution of the family in modern society.

The three contrasting models of social policy represent different criteria for making choices. We analyse the implications of Model A in the next chapter and refer to it and the other models in a number of other chapters later in the book.

3

Laissez-Faire and Stigma

In this chapter we consider an extreme view of social policy: that it is morally indefensible to force or compel some individuals, irrespective of their circumstances, wishes or beliefs, to give help, in cash or in kind (and thus to live at a lower standard of living) to beneficiaries whose incomes and circumstances have not been inquired into. It is the case for minimum government, central and local, maximum liberation from State intervention, a residual role for (preferably) a voluntary social policy, and maximum permission (or freedom) for the individual to act according to his own conscience and to spend his own money as he wishes in the private market without let or interference from officials and bureaucrats 'who cannot know best'. This, it is argued, is the moral case for the Residual Welfare Model.

The term *laissez-faire* was coined by a group of French political economists known as Physiocrats. The Physiocrats criticised the so-called Mercantilist System under which the government controlled the manufacture and pricing of goods, the location of industries, and the movement of trade, with the aim of securing a favourable balance of trade for the country. The Physiocrats, as their name indicates – the Greek word *physis* means 'nature' – favoured a more spontaneous, natural and less artificial industrial and commercial system. Hence, *laissez-faire* meant 'let people move around as they please'.

Adam Smith was influenced by some of the arguments of the Physiocrats when, in *The Wealth of Nations* (1776), he argued that national prosperity is more likely to result from allowing goods to be freely produced and exchanged than from controlling production and exchange by governmental means.

The argument, in short, was a plea for a more natural, spontaneous, communal, liberated society. There are echoes of it today in the writings of Marcuse, Professor Friedman of Chicago and others. It is summed up by Professor Acton in a recent book *The Morals of Markets*, which is clearly addressed to the young and to those who believe that natural justice is equated with consumerism (e.g. the consumer is king). It is, not surprisingly, sponsored by the Institute of Economic Affairs in London and embodied and summarised in most of the books, pamphlets and articles published by the Institute over a broad field of what we have conventionally called 'the social services'. Fundamentally, it re-states the moral case for individual freedom of choice – in a sense it is a Rights Charter or an individualistic private Welfare Rights philosophy.

The argument for freedom – particularly freedom from the exercise of discretionary power by Government bureaucracies – is not confined by Professor Acton to markets in which goods are bought, sold and exchanged. He develops his 'ethical explorations' and applies them to subsidised public housing, rent control, social security, medical care, state education from the nursery school to the university, and other sectors of welfare commonly thought of as social policy institutions. In these and other areas he rejects the notion of bureaucratic planning (change is inevitable and must be left to take care of itself). 'Competitive markets are likely to do less harm than centralised economic planning and to give more scope for intellectual and moral excellence.'[1] Men will be freer (like nature), thoughts will be freer, participation in society and community action will be more spontaneous.

[1] Acton, H. B., *The Morals of Markets: an ethical exploration*, Longmans, London, 1971.

To this moral case for private markets in social policy and individual freedom two reservations can be made at this stage. The first is that men (and women) should be free not to work. But if they choose not to do so, should they morally expect to have their needs met by the community – through social security, welfare payments or the Supplementary Benefits Commission, or in other ways?

This *laissez-faire* thesis is in many respects fundamentally different from the ideology of the Poor Law (Amendment) Act of 1834 – one objective of which (as part of the puritan ethic) was to drive men to work or into the workhouse. Thus, Professor Acton takes a quite different position from, for example, that of Professor Richard Cloward and Frances Fox-Piven in their book *Regulating the Poor*.[1] Using historical and contemporary materials from the USA and England – beginning with the English statutes about beggars in 1488–9 and ending with Welfare Rights litigation in Harlem in 1969 – Cloward and Fox-Piven discuss the role of public assistance in forcing men (and unmarried mothers) to work and in regulating the lives and policing the conduct of the poor:

'... The much more fundamental problem with which relief reform seeks to cope is the erosion of the work role. When large numbers of people come to subsist on the dole, many of them spurning what little low-wage work may exist, those of the poor and near-poor who continue to work are inevitably affected. From their perspective, the ready availability of relief payments (often at levels only slightly below prevailing wages) undermines their chief claim to social status: namely, that although poor they nevertheless earn their livelihood. If most of them react with anger, others react by asking, "Why work?" The *danger* thus arises that swelling numbers of the working poor will choose to go on relief.

'Moreover, when attachments to the work role deteriorate, so

---

[1] Cloward, R. and Fox-Piven, F., *Regulating the Poor: the functions of public welfare*, Tavistock Publications, London, 1971.

Social Policy

do attachments to the family, especially the attachment of men to their families. For all practical purposes, the relief check becomes a surrogate for the male breadwinner. The resulting family breakdown and loss of control over the young is usually signified by the spread of certain forms of *disorder* – for example, *school failure*, crime and addiction. In other words, the mere giving of relief, while it mutes the more disruptive outbreaks of civil disorder (such as rioting), does little to stem the fragmentation of lower-class life, even while it further undermines the patterns of work by which the lower class is ordinarily regulated. When all of this becomes clear to élites, the stage is set for the restoration of the work-maintaining function of the relief system.'[1]

As Cloward and Fox-Piven see it in the current crisis of Welfare in the United States, there is no prospect of reform in the welfare field; no future for social policies in this area. Their answer is also (like Acton's) less government and less public bureaucracy and a resurrection of the work ethic in the private market-place. Their basic plea therefore is for changes in *economic policy* and for more emphasis on economic growth which would make more jobs available. Their assumption is that work – any sort of paid work – exercises much less of a regulatory (or policing) control over the lives and behaviour of the poor than any conceivable changes in public assistance in the USA.

The second comment which can be made about Professor Acton's book (and, indeed, the whole concept of the Residual Welfare Model) is that it has nothing to say about one of the great issues of our times – the problems of race relations, ethnic conflict and racial discrimination. One can only assume Acton believes that the private market is more likely to provide solutions (like the movement for Black Capitalism in the United States) than intervention by the Government in the

---

[1] *Ibid.*, p. 343. The italics have been added to the original text to stress the moral overtones.

form of social policy action. But all the evidence, so far as Britain is concerned, is against him. Governmental bureaucracies in this country have a better record in respect to the recruitment, employment, post-entry training and promotion of black people than private enterprise – particularly most of the insurance companies and of the mass media. Not one single case of alleged racial discrimination has been brought against the National Health Service or the Social Security system (including the Supplementary Benefit Commission) since the Act of 1968. It does not, of course, follow that no racial discrimination has taken place. But the situation is strikingly different in the USA – particularly in the area of private medical care.

Indeed, Professor Cohn[1] has shown that the private sector in total has failed to make a contribution to the problem of the disadvantaged – and particularly the black disadvantaged – in the USA. After the Watts, Detroit and Newark riots of 1965–7 great pressure (plus financial subsidies) was brought to bear by the Federal Government on American business to employ, train, educate, re-train, rehabilitate and provide social services for the disadvantaged: school drop-outs, unemployed young people, handicapped men and women, people with prison records and so forth. Professor Cohn documents and analyses the performance of the private market since 1967 in this critical area of ethnic relations. He concludes that despite the employment of masses of industrial psychologists, group trainers, 'sensitivity' consultants from universities, counsellors and other breeds of consultants, the record is one of almost total failure. The situation, he says, is getting worse. For example, unemployment in the Watts section of Los Angeles rose from 10·2 per cent at the time of the 1965 riots to 16·2 per cent at the end of 1969 and the jobless rate among black women nearly doubled during the same period.[2]

With the advent of the race relations issue in modern society, social policy has acquired (or it can be argued should acquire) a

[1] Cohn, J., *The Conscience of the Corporation*, Johns Hopkins Press, Baltimore, 1971.
[2] *Ibid.*, p. 106.

new function – a community relations or non-discriminatory integrative function. This can have a positive role – the promotion of harmonious community relations. It can also have a negative role – the prevention of a sense, and a fact, of racial discrimination. It is now (or should be) an objective of social policy to build the identity of a person around some community with which he is associated. It is this function which is one of the characteristics which distinguishes social policy from economic policy and the role of Government from the role of the private market. Voluntary hospitals in the United States, for example, have public wards for indigents which tend to be full of black people. This can be contrasted with the integrated wards and outpatient departments of British hospitals under the National Health Service.

All this is relevant to the problem of defining and redefining the concept and changing roles of social policy. And it is also relevant to the debate about universalist and selective social services. The failure of American welfare and social policies to deal with these issues of race relations and poverty has led to a movement for 'the reprivatisation of Government'. Indeed, the moral questions raised by Acton are no mere theoretical musings of a professor of philosophy. His conception of natural justice is being applied in practice in the USA. It is variously called 'the reprivatisation of governmental functions' or 'the substitution of official bureaucracies with the pluralism, freedom, adaptability and community focus' that is said to characterise non-governmental agencies (charitable and profit-making) in the area of the social services.

The basis of the case for 'reprivatisation' was advanced in 1969 by Professor Peter Drucker.[1] His argument is that virtually all non-military governmental functions should be 'reprivatised' or returned to the market place. By this he means that they should be delegated to or contracted out to autonomous private or quasi-public organisations who would

[1] Drucker, P., *The Age of Discontinuity*, Heinemann, London, 1969.

charge what the traffic could bear. He argues that government, especially central or Federal government, is too big, too bureaucratic, too rigid, too remote from the grass-roots, too unresponsive to consumer demands and welfare rights, too costly, monolithic and unadaptable – to name only a few of his assertions. Government, he concludes, is by its very nature unfit for the effective delivery of goods and services and should, therefore, be freed from these burdens in order to concentrate on a leadership role. This role he compares to that of the conductor of an orchestra, although it is not clear who pays the musicians and who benefits from the music.

The case argued by Drucker, Friedman, Acton and others is today being translated into social policy action. One example is in the field of elementary education:

'GARY, Ind. – Banneker School is one of 36 elementary schools in this grimy industrial city, but it differs from the others. If its 840 pupils don't master reading and maths as well as others their age across the country, the school system gets its money back.

'That's because Banneker is run by a private company, Behavioral Research Laboratories Inc. (BRL) of Palo Alto, Calif., under contract to the Gary board of education. The school district pays the company about $670,000 a year, or $800 for each student, the district's cost of educating each pupil last year. Out of that the company pays for teachers' salaries, for educational materials and even for rent of the school building. It must refund the full $800 for every child who doesn't perform up to national standards in reading and maths at the end of the three-year agreement. Anything left over is BRL's profit.

'Gary is the only US city that has turned over an entire school to a company to run on a money-back guarantee basis, but many others are trying the concept on a more limited scale. More than 40 school districts, including those in New York, Philadelphia, Dallas and Seattle, have entered into so-called performance contracts covering some 40,000 students this year, and the US Office of Education estimates that an additional 150 systems are studying the concept. A year ago only one such contract existed, covering 350 students in Texarkana, Ark.

'Minds, Not Machines

The practice is controversial. The 228,000-member American Federation of Teachers views it as a threat to job security. Some educators object because they believe the practice will focus teaching efforts on reading and maths where performance is easily measured, and that music, art, social studies and other important areas will be neglected. Others fear that companies will turn schools into something akin to factories.

'Performance contractors aren't using any teaching techniques that are revolutionary or that schools themselves haven't tried. They rely heavily on individualized instruction with each child proceeding at his own pace, not that of a class. They group children by ability, not age. Teachers work in teams, and parents are hired to help in the classrooms.

'The school managers's job is to plan and organize the educational program, keep performance records to see how the pupils are doing, and in short, to see that the system works. For this, BRL brought in a former systems analyst for space projects at Lockheed Corp., Donald G. Kendrick, because it wanted someone with industry experience in setting goals, devising systems to reach them and meeting deadlines.

'The Child as a Component

"This project is like building a missile," he says. "Every child is a component: you have to keep an eye on each one to see how he's functioning."[1]

The system is akin to the system of 'payment-by-results' for teachers in the elementary schools of England in the nineteenth

---

[1] James, R. D., 'Three R's Inc.', *Wall Street Journal*, 2 June 1971.

century (though in a more sophisticated form including the stimulation of the profit motive). Both systems relied (or rely) on performance in the three R's which is measurable, quantifiable, and thus can be exposed to the presumed stimulation of the profit motive. The American arguments in favour of introducing criteria of profit into the educational system are that (a) teachers work harder (b) fewer teachers are needed (c) parents are brought into participation and (d) the teaching profession is brought under control and thus there is less professional bias in favour of the bright, higher I.Q. white child.[1]

A second example is of the 'reprivatisation' of hospitals. This takes the form of the purchase of voluntary and charitable hospitals (and in some cases public hospitals) by profit-making corporations. In March 1970 there were in the USA over fifty corporations operating profit-making hospitals and many more running nursing and convalescent homes for profit. In addition to buying up local community hospitals these corporations are rapidly building new ones. This development of introducing profit criteria into the treatment of hospital care has been increasing at a remarkably fast rate in the last two to three years. Financially, it has been so successful that one of the largest corporations, American Medical Enterprises Corporation, is now extending its operations overseas – to London, Holland and other countries. A similar process of 'reprivatisation' is also taking place in the provision of ambulance services. (In Chicago, where ambulances are run for profit, it is said that it is more profitable to remove the dead to undertakers – who pay a higher price – than the living to hospitals.) Clinical and bacteriological laboratories are also to a very large extent operated by private enterprise.

In part, all these developments in the area of private social policy in the USA (in elementary education, hospitals,

---

[1] For a later critical view, see, General Accounting Office, *Evaluation of the Office of Economic Opportunities' Performance Contracting Experiment*, 8 May 1973 CGAO index No. B-1305-15.

laboratories, ambulances and so forth) have been encouraged politically, on the extreme right and the radical left, by the increasing critique of authority – and particularly authority in the shape of government. Government is said or seen to represent bureaucratic power, the denial of consumer rights and freedom; in short, it is a monolithic establishment.

These paradoxical reactions in those sectors that Western society has conventionally called 'social services' raise what Isaiah Berlin described as 'the central question of politics – the question of obedience and coercion. Why should I (or anyone) obey anyone else? Why should I not live as I like?'[1] Why should I not 'contract out' of 'giving relationships'? These questions are discussed in *The Gift Relationship*[2] but they are also raised by the trend towards minimum government and the 'reprivatisation' of the social services sector or what, in this country and in a different context, is called 'hiving-off' to other agencies, profit-making and quasi-public.

The consequences of 'living as I like', of spending one's own money, of retreating from accountable government, are difficult to assess. The middle- and upper-income groups, in Britain and the USA, may be exploited for profit-making purposes by contracting-out and using private medical care or private pension schemes. They probably are, because of the higher administrative, advertising and selling costs in the private market. Nevertheless, apart from all other considerations of freedom of choice, privacy and amenity, the profit margins may be lower than the redistributive costs (in taxation and a variety of complex mechanisms) of being compelled or coerced to pay for social services provided by a government bureaucracy for poorer people.

Private enterprise social service institutions have to operate on the principle of excluding the 'bad risks' and the social casualties of change. Thus, private occupational schemes

[1] Berlin, I., *Four Essays on Liberty*, Oxford University Press, London, 1969.
[2] Titmuss, R. M., *The Gift Relationship*, Allen & Unwin, London, 1971.

exclude the chronically sick, the disabled, the elderly, the mentally handicapped, new entrants, most categories of women – especially unmarried mothers – and so on. Private medical institutions similarly exclude 'the bad risks', the over-80s, the indigent and so-called charitable cases. What are called 'money-losers' by profit-making hospitals in the USA include obstetrics, paediatrics, emergency departments, medical training departments and, particularly, the indigents. As one executive director of one of the largest American proprietary hospitals put it: 'why should a solvent citizen be penalised for falling sick by being forced, through a hospital bill padded by about fifteen per cent, to pay more than his taxpayer's share for the community's indigent care?'[1]

Excluding the 'bad risks' has other beneficial consequences; there is said to be less bureaucracy because fewer officials are needed if an institution does not have to deal with all the complex equity considerations entailed in providing services for poor people (a price tariff replaces far more complex Welfare Manuals and Regulations). A second beneficial effect is that problems of 'stigma' are excluded from that particular institution. You do not have to cope in a single hospital with pay-bed patients and public patients as the British National Health Service does. Nor do you, as another by-product, have to cope to the same degree with issues of race relations because few black people in the USA can afford to pay the price of private medical care in hospital (now probably approaching something like £500 per week).

The word 'stigma' originally meant a mark physically branded on a slave or a criminal. What it is generally taken to refer to today is an imputation attaching to a person's reputation or standing. To stigmatise a person then is to describe him or his behaviour in culturally offensive or unacceptable terms, for example as a coward, a layabout, a racist, an Uncle Tom, a failure, a C-streamer and so on. Of course, a good deal turns on

---

[1] Quoted in *Medical Economics*, 30 March 1970.

who is talking (or thinking) about whom. High-born Hindus in a caste society – and in Britain – think of Muslims as work-shy and dirty. Poor whites in Notting Hill describe West Indian mothers as neglectful when they go out to work. Manual workers – particularly in the North of England and Scotland – think of university students as 'pampered lay-abouts'. Civil servants, according to many businessmen, are bureaucrats, inveterate tea-drinkers and makers of red-tape.

There are certain aspects of what one can call 'the process of institutional stigmatising' which are relevant in a wider context. First, the concept itself is as elusive and complex as other key concepts like class, alienation, participation, demo-cracy, poverty and so forth. In part, it is what we think it is. In part, it is what others think it is. In part, it is our (and society's) objectification of a man's role in life. If men and women come to think of (and feel) themselves as inferior persons, subor-dinated persons, then in part they stigmatise themselves, and in part they are reflecting what other people think or say about them.

Some of the difficulties of understanding and interpreting the psychology of these inter-connected concepts like 'stigma' and 'alienation' are spelt out by Mészáros,[1] who discusses the notions of man's estrangement from work, from nature and from himself. Goffman[2] develops other aspects and speculates about the effects of social services in the United States. He takes mental institutions as an example of imposing stigma or 'spoiling identity'. He argues that the longer the period of dependency persists, the more likely the dependent is to re-define his total social life in terms of the stigma. People adapt to handicap, physical and mental, they adapt to poverty, they adapt to old age. There is some truth in the statement that if society – the mass media, political consensus, a younger generation, occupational pension schemes or what you will –

[1] Mészáros, I., *Marx's Theory of Alienation*, Merlin Press, London, 1970.
[2] Goffman, E., *Stigma: notes on the management of spoiled identity*, Penguin, Harmondsworth, 1968.

defines old age as anyone over 50 then, in time, people come to accept a dependent status and the so-called 'sanction of stigma'.

The trouble, however, with Goffman and many other American writers on the subject of 'stigma' and social policy is that they are extraordinarily parochial. They generalise and develop sophisticated theories on the basis of American values and mythologies about independence, work, thrift, private enterprise, the self-made man, the self-made President. Thus, indirectly or by implication, governmental bureaucracies are inferior, stigmatising forms of coercion. It is a social process of stigmatisation. Those who make use of the public services are self-confessed failures. In particular, those who apply for Welfare aid – for public assistance – are said to feel 'pauperised'. And because they feel that way (and are socialised to think accordingly) they therefore (or so the argument runs) have to believe that others on welfare (but not themselves) are 'chisellers, cheaters, welfare bums and abusers of the system'. And so, theoretically, it goes on spiralling. The more that the welfare system (or public services in general) is said or believed to stigmatise, the more those who staff the system may think that it is their function to stigmatise. The attitudes of both claimants and staff reinforce each other; they create what they fear – or what others want them to fear. It seems that the American middle-classes (including many American academics) need scapegoats to sustain their values. And the welfare system is a scapegoat *par excellence*. To a lesser extent this is true in Britain of the Supplementary Benefits Commission and Social Services Departments.

It does not, however, follow that one can theorise or generalise in any universal sense from American values and experiences, any more than one can generalise about the effects of the caste system in India. What it feels like to be a public assistance recipient is – on all the evidence – very different in Copenhagen, Oslo, Amsterdam and Stockholm. Nor is it necessarily true that 'Public Services may have a greater propensity to stigmatise.'[1] Greater than what? Private enterprise? Private markets? We are not told.

What may be true is that 'Public services may have a greater propensity to be criticised' and for many obvious reasons. First, they are accountable services. Second, more information about them is made public. Third, more research has been carried out on public markets than on private markets. Fourth, there is today much more money to be made by the mass media (and more academics turned journalists) from criticising the public services than criticising private enterprise. And, fifth, to public opinion (as well as writers on Max Weber) 'bureaucracy' means Government – not ICI or Marks and Spencer or the Prudential Insurance Company.

Nevertheless, despite the criticisms for over twenty years – from the British Medical Association and other quarters – it is questionable whether the great majority of people who have used the National Health Service have felt 'dependent' and 'stigmatised'. The fact that the service is 'universalist' in scope – or is thought to be so – is one factor. But there are many others which are discussed later in this book.

[1] Pinker, R. A., *Social Theory and Social Policy*, Heinemann, London, 1971, p. 175.

4

Social Administration and Social Welfare

All the difficulties in attempts to define 'Social Policy' arise also in the use of such concepts and terms as 'The Welfare State', social welfare, the social services, and social administration. We may regard the labels 'social services' and 'social welfare' as broadly synonymous. But many of the reservations and qualifications applied above to social policy can also be applied to these terms.

When one examines the over twenty different definitions of these terms made in a number of different countries in Europe and in North America, one finds that they all vary to some degree depending on the particular culture, history and value systems of the countries concerned. And they all vary according to the reasons why a definition is being sought. Some, of course, place more emphasis on trade union or voluntary services (wholly or partly financed by non-governmental agencies); some give more prominence to *personal* services which involve the use of professional staff (social workers, doctors and others) in the delivery of services; some refer mainly to income services like social security and similar transfer payments; and some relate social services to social problems. Thus, Professor Pusic of Yugoslavia stated: 'Social welfare is the sum of measures developed by a society in order to cope with its social problems.'[1]

[1] Pusic, E., *Report to the Secretary General on a Reappraisal of the United Nations Social Service Programme*, 1965 (E/CNS/AC12/L3/Add.I).

What then is a 'social problem'? Merton and Nisbet offer one answer:

'Just about everyone has at heart a gross conception of "social problems". Unsought but undeniable troubles in society, social conflicts and confusions usually described as the "social crisis of our time", the victimizing of people by social institutions that put them at a disadvantage in life, crime, curable but uncured disease, the socially unauthorized use of violence – all these and more are caught up in what most of us ordinarily mean by the term "social problem".'[1]

Poverty, in the form of inadequate education, income, housing and other forms of social inequality, is not, you will note, included as a 'social problem'.

If Pusic is right in his interpretation in his UN Report then we must conclude that there are two significantly different concepts of 'the social services'. One sees them as being concerned with social problems and social pathology; with adjusting and rehabilitating individuals and families to the values and norms of society. This concept is close to our Model A of social policy, the *Residual Welfare Model*, one of whose objectives (we have seen) is to function as a means of social control and to maintain law and order. The other, and markedly different concept, sees the social services as instruments to provide for certain specified needs in society regardless of value judgements about individuals and families as to whether or not they constitute social problems. This concept is more closely related to our third Model – Model C, the *Institutional Redistributive Model of Social Policy*.

These are some of the difficulties of defining social policy, social welfare and the social services. There is, of course, much more that could be said about these difficulties, but there is an intellectual limit to the amount of theorising about definitions

[1] Merton, R. K. and Nisbet, R. A., *Contemporary Social Problems*, Harcourt, New York, 1961, p. 701.

that is of educational use in, so to speak, a conceptual value vacuum. A stage is reached in which we feel the need to ask: for what purposes are definitions required? What are we trying to measure, compare or evaluate? To understand better what it is all about have not we in the end to ask concrete questions about specific policies and services rather than to generalise broadly about 'social policy' in the abstract?

But how does the study of social administration relate to these issues? What is it and why do we study it? In the popular mind, some people think that 'Social Administration' has something to do with administering an office (how to file letters and so forth); with techniques and methods; some people connect it vaguely with social work or 'doing good' (why is it thought to be academically inferior to be educated to 'do good'?); and some people connect it with local government and parish councils.

This problem of defining and explaining subjects and areas of interest in the broad areas of the social sciences as a whole is not peculiar to 'Social Administration'. It applies no less – though in different ways – to political science (is there a science of politics?); to international relations (is this a training for journalism?); to public administration (can administration be taught?); and to sociology (what does a professional socio-logist actually do – compared, for example, with the role of the professional economist in HM Treasury?).

'Social Policy' and 'Social Administration' are often con-fused just as we all at different times are confused between ends and means, objectives and routes, fundamentalism and incre-mentalism (a current American debate), utopia and the means of travel.

Social policy is basically about *choices* between conflicting political objectives and goals and how they are formulated; what constitutes the good society or that part of a good society which culturally distinguishes between the needs and aspira-tions of social man in contradiction to the needs and aspira-tions of economic man. The study of Social Administration is, on the other hand, largely concerned with the study of certain human organisations and formal structures (and choices between them) which deliver or provide what we call 'social services'. There are some writers, like T. H. Marshall, who refer to this area as 'social engineering'.[1] Others to the far left of Marshall have described it as 'social plumbing'. However, whether one approves or disapproves of these mechanistic-manipulative physical models, what some of these writers have in mind is the analysis of the methods by which available resources (in cash and in kind) are brought to bear on socially recognised needs.

But the problems involved in the study of Social Administration are not wholly problems of method. There is a value component in discussions about selectivity and universality – a subject (if it is a subject) which cannot be debated at all without considering both aims and methods. There is the issue of the merits and demerits of positive discrimination, integration and segregation; and beyond the question of how a service should be conveyed, there is the problem of ensuring that it is in fact delivered – that it reaches those citizens who need it most. Those who study or work in the social services (public servants, administrators, professional staff) are not the only people who in recent years have had to think about these problems of policy (objectives) and delivery (means).

Social scientists of all kinds have been led by the logic of their studies to examine human organisations more closely. Political scientists concerned with power, economists concerned with the distribution of scarce resources, sociologists concerned with the structure and development of society, and psychologists concerned with human motivation and behaviour must all at some point examine the organisations through which power is exercised, the organisations in which decisions about the allocation of resources are made and implemented, the organisations that go far to determine the structure

---

[1] Marshall, T. H., *Social Policy*, Hutchinson, University Library, London, 1965.

of our society and the perceptions and aspirations of its members. Thus administration is not a self-contained specialism; it is the meeting point and common concern of all these disciplines. Indeed it is the concern of all who live in an industrial, urban country. For if 'administration' is the management of human organisations, then all of us – as employees and customers, patients and pupils, voters and taxpayers – are familiar with many aspects of it; and in a country which devotes about a sixth of its gross national product to social services, 'social' administration constitutes a major part of this familiar process.

The administration process consists of a series, or many related series, of actions taken by individuals and groups. These people collaborate with each other in a reasonably systematic and predictable manner, they treat each other in distinctive ways and play specialised parts in the administrative story: that is to say their behaviour is 'organised'. *Organisation* is again an abstract concept; it consists of the specialised roles of each person concerned in the development to be studied, and the relationships between these roles. Like the tasks and processes of administration, it may be discussed in terms of its 'manifest', 'assumed', 'extant' or 'requisite' content. Like the processes, too, it is not something concrete that lies around waiting to be discovered: features of organisation that are relevant for one task may be irrelevant for others, and people concerned with different tasks will often describe administrative organisation in very different terms, even though all of them are employed in the same agency.

It has been argued – or assumed – by some writers on the social services that the work of administrators (central, regional and local) is no different from that of administrators and managers in what is called private enterprise. Hence, the current emphasis on Management (or Management By Objectives) in place of administration.

This assumption should be criticised on three grounds. First, the objectives of social services (from university education to social work) are not to make profits and to administer prices –

unlike private markets. <u>They are concerned with delivering</u>
<u>and providing services to meet publicly acknowledged needs</u>
<u>which markets or the family cannot, or should not, or will not,</u>
<u>meet.</u> It follows, therefore, that the end-results of the work of
administrators and professionals in the social services are less
susceptible (if susceptible at all) to quantification and measure-
ment than the work of managers in the private sector. We
cannot easily measure the effects of particular delivery systems
in the satisfaction of education, medical care, child guidance,
adoption procedures, cash transfer payments and so forth.

In a recent Report, the British Department of Education
conceded that criteria for the output of education would be
slow and laborious to work out, and its efforts at programme
budgeting so far were limited to a rearrangement of inputs
rather than an attempt to measure final objectives:[1] 'The
reactions of the local authority witnesses indicated, however,
that they found it difficult to think of output budgeting as
having a serious contribution to make in the educational field
in the absence of a valid means of quantifying the long-term
benefits of education to the community.'[2] Certain authorities
were beginning to develop programme budgeting, but 'the
views which the subcommittee heard from local authorities on
this subject were distinctly sceptical'.[3] The department was
hopeful of finding suitable measures for 'intermediate output',
such as numbers in various levels of education, but Mr Hudson
told the MPs that to assign values to outputs 'is both very
difficult and cannot possibly be free from controversy. To take
an obvious sort of example, you have to be able to compare the
provision of two years' nursery education for a three-year-old
child with the provision of two years' post-graduate study for
somebody reading for a Ph.D.'[4]

[1] *Second Report from the House of Commons Expenditure Committee* (*Education and
Arts Sub-committee*), House of Commons Paper 545, 1971, p. x, para. 21.

[2] *Ibid.*, p. xi, para. 21.

[3] *Ibid.*, p. x, para. 20.

[4] *Ibid.*, p. 229, Q. 1002. Mr Hudson was Deputy Under Secretary, Department of
Education and Science.

There are few criteria of success (though there are negative ones in the form of failure) in assessing the performance of social service systems. What is, for example, success for the Director of a Social Services Department, the Manager of a Supplementary Benefits or public assistance office, a general practitioner, a probation officer, a hostel manager for homeless people or discharged manic depressives?

Social research in a variety of fields has shown that we cannot equate changes in demand – explicit expressed demand – with the effectiveness or efficiency of a social service agency. Increased turnover (or productivity), 'getting people off the books', increasing charges or other deterrent or rationing devices, closing the case file, and so forth are not necessarily criteria of successful performance. This can be best shown by illustrations.

What is *success* for a mental hospital? The new drugs have resulted in a more rapid turnover of cases and more patients discharged to 'community care'. *Success* for the hospital may mean more demands on other agencies. Many of these patients end up in welfare institutions for the single homeless which were not designed to cater for this type of need. Here we see the connections between the work and performance of different parts of the social services. What is wrongly assumed to be success for one agency may be failure for another.

What is *success* in policies to provide cash to maintain deserted wives? Can we just look at whether the money was received and ignore the consequences on others of providing the money. In 1971, the Supplementary Benefits Commission spent £100 million on supporting deserted wives because of the failure of husbands to provide for their wives and children (and the failure of the courts to make them provide). Of the £100 million only 9 per cent was ultimately recovered from the husbands. In Sweden, the corresponding agencies managed to recover 40 per cent of what was spent on the maintenance of deserted wives. Britain was less successful because all the information available to all public authorities is not used in the search: we accept the principle that, in general, information given by the public to government for one purpose should not be used for another. In Sweden the process of searching is much more systematic. They accept computerised checking and a data bank society. It is hard to hide in Sweden. Even if the father does succeed in hiding, his car can be impounded. Is this Swedish example a measure of *success? Success* in making husbands pay or in sending them to prison can mean a failure to preserve privacy and the freedom to disappear for a majority of citizens.

What is *success* in running a general practice? In London 65 per cent of general practitioners use deputising services to handle calls from patients at night or at week-ends. In practice this means that the doctor who visits the patient's home has had no previous contact with the patient and has no access to the patient's medical record. The doctors doing this work are usually young and inexperienced. For these reasons they tend to 'play it safe' and refer a high proportion of patients to the hospitals as casualty or emergency cases. Not only is this an incorrect use of the hospital's resources but it is disturbing for patients to be admitted to hospital unnecessarily. The general practitioners concerned may, however, claim that they are *successfully* running their practices as fewer demands are being made for their services.

A second factor or principle which distinguishes social administration from administration in the market place is the need for social administrators to have far more knowledge about human behaviour and human needs. Scientific advances and the contribution of the behavioural sciences in recent decades have not only added to our understanding of human needs but have shown that these needs are often multiple, many-sided, complex and prolonged. Social administrators (as well as such professions as medicine, teaching, nursing and social work) now require to be 'sensitised' to the multiplicity and many-sidedness of human needs. In a sense, this is what we mean when we talk about the problems of co-ordination, social diagnoses, welfare referral, evaluation, and so forth.

By contrast, the private market in consumption goods does not have to co-ordinate the purchases of a particular consumer of refrigerators and saucepans. Its purpose is to sell such articles separately and success is measured by sales and profits. Some sectors of private enterprise do of course study their markets but the market is for each individual item considered in isolation from other items. One conclusion that can be drawn from this analysis is that unlike those operating in private markets, social administrators (and their allied professions) require more education and more training, particularly in the social sciences.

A third distinguishing factor – and one that is linked to the education/training principle – involves consideration once again of the issues of confidentiality, ethical codes of behaviour and public accountability. Because people cannot 'shop around' for social work support, medical care, education and cash assistance (at least in Britain) to the same extent as they can for shoes or cabbages in the private market, these issues thus become much more important. What some economists describe as the 'disciplines of private markets' are not applicable or appropriate in the public sector of the social services. Other kinds of disciplines have to be fashioned – more education, training and in-training; an incorruptible, secure civil service, developing its own codes of behaviour, rule-making and procedures, and continually preoccupied with problems of equity and fairness as between one citizen and another; the use of 'quality controls' through Parliament, investigating committees, research, inspectorates, pressure groups and so forth.[1] In short, if social services are to be delivered effectively, equitably and humanely, more and better educated social administrators are required.

[1] For a discussion of quality controls and the responsibilities of the Supplementary Benefits Commission, see Titmuss, R. M., 'Welfare Rights: law and discretion', *Political Quarterly*, April 1971.

Fundamentally, then, it is a manpower problem. And although at first sight this may seem to represent issues of method, organisation, staffing (or 'social engineering'), there are at bottom crucial political choices involved. More civil servants, administrators, doctors, teachers, social workers, nurses and many other occupational categories means more government – not less government, less State intervention, minimum government or, as some would say, 'fewer bureaucrats'. More government thus means more taxation, more redistribution and less private consumption. And to attract, recruit and staff the social services also raises competitive issues of pay, rewards and career earnings.[1]

At present, the backbone of the administration of the social services is the staff in the clerical officer and executive officer grades of the civil service and the equivalent grades in local government. How do the rewards of bank clerks and insurance clerks who have responsible but largely routine work compare for given educational qualifications with the rewards of the staff of supplementary benefits offices dealing with the socially handicapped and social inadequates? Not only are the rewards of supplementary benefit staff relatively inadequate but they are also subject to military 'posting' (another discipline) and compulsory overtime (yet another form of 'posting'). For years these offices have been understaffed while banks have often been over-staffed, particularly on new university campuses. For example, there are bank branches at the University of Kent just outside Canterbury to save students the journey into the city. Or, to take another example, in 1970 the four major banks spent more than £200,000 in advertising to university students (on the assumption that students today will be the financial élites of tomorrow).[2] By contrast, the Conservative Government spent £150,000 on advertising the take-up campaign for Family Income Supple-

---

[1] For a general discussion of relative pay, see Wootton, B., *The Social Foundations of Wage Policy*, Allen & Unwin, London, 1955.
[2] *The Times*, 15 July 1971.

ments. Or compare the rewards of nursing staff in hospitals for the mentally handicapped with the salaries of administrative officers for university student unions.[1]

These are some of the distinguishing characteristics which differentiate the role and responsibilities of administrators in the social services from those of administrators (or managers) in the private sector. Only within limits is it feasible to separate Policy (objectives) from Administration (means or delivery) as a branch of study. Whether we are analysing education, housing, medical care or social security, there comes a point when the two overlap and interact. Administrative methods or delivery processes or organisational structures influence policies and vice versa. Administrative manpower shortages can mean, for example, the adoption in policy terms of more rationing devices and different end-results in the distribution of the command-over-resources of individuals through time. Social problems, when analysed, rarely follow a simple means-ends pattern. Each end is or may be a means to further ends. Thus, when one analyses a specific social problem, the adoption (as a matter of policy) of a particular organisational structure means the reformulation or revaluation of ends. What, for example, are the ends – or goals – of local authority social services departments?

As a subject of study in the field of further education, it can thus be argued that Social Policy and Administration constitutes a synthesis – an interdisciplinary way of studying certain social institutions, problems and processes in society. This subject area does not, therefore, rest to the same extent as, for example, economics on a comprehensive body of theoretical knowledge. Nor does it exist to describe a technical body of information for professional training – as do, for example, most law faculties in Britain. It does not claim to be a distinctive, separate discipline. For some of its theory and some of its concepts, Social Policy and Administration draws on

---

[1] Essex University offered a salary up to £2,000 in 1971 for a graduate administrative officer. (*The Times*, 3 September 1971.)

economics, on political science, on sociology, on psychology, on moral philosophy and related disciplines. For its methods of study it leans heavily on statistical theory, social survey techniques and history. In recent years, the subject (in its various branches of study like social security and medical care) has been drawing on these theories and concepts, refining them, extending them, and adapting them to further our understanding of the roles and functions of the social services in contemporary society.

Basically, it may be said that the subject is concerned with an ill-defined but nevertheless recognisable territory – the structure, history, organisation, practices and principles of collective action (economic, social, political) falling within the area of social welfare. It is not, therefore, concerned with methodology for its own sake but only insofar as methods of analysis (statistical, sociological or philosophical) can shed light on particular institutions or systems. By its nature, and because most people who are interested in the subject are concerned with social change and social reform, it tends to be problem-oriented – not because of pathology but because the subject is about social choices in the allocation of scarce resources, choices, for example, between Equity and Equality. Because it is problem-oriented, Social Policy and Administration cannot isolate itself from the broader context of society itself. Hence, we have consciously to see development and change in collective action (in terms of policies for welfare) against the historical backdrop of broader economic, social and political factors. It calls, in short, for a particular focus of vision in seeking to study certain segments of social life and behaviour.

We study Social Policy and Administration – and this is a personal view – because, in looking at the state of the world today, we are concerned about social justice in many of its manifestations, and because such study may help us a little to understand better certain aspects of complex modern societies. It is insufficiently recognised in many universities that some of the great issues of social relations today are not susceptible to analysis and understanding by any *one* social science discipline alone. In part, this has happened because we have compartmentalised and departmentalised knowledge about man in society. 'Not only,' said John Ruskin over a hundred years ago, 'is there but one way of *doing* things rightly, but there is only one way of seeing them, and that is seeing the whole of them.'[1]

Teachers generally leave to students the task of relating knowledge in one discipline to that in another. While they may declare their faith in the generic, the whole, and the multidisciplinary – whether they are talking about diagnosis, learning, social action or planning – nevertheless, they want to specialise and to define more clearly their own professional, administrative, social work or teaching roles. They want to be more certain about themselves and their identity in an increasingly complex society. It is indeed a comfort to acquire and cultivate one small allotment of skill and knowledge in the vastness of the knowable so that one can feel a little more at home. To these internal pressures there are added external ones. Everyone wants others to be sure about their identity, role and functions, for identity and specialisation are linked to status. And professional people, whether they be teachers, doctors or social workers, are pre-eminently people with status problems. But there is one small compensation. Unlike some who teach in other fields, those who teach social administration do not have continually to look over their shoulders and ask themselves whether they are behaving, teaching or researching like professional social administrators. There is no such animal.

[1] Ruskin, J., *The Two Paths*, Lecture 2, in *Sesame and Lilies, the Two Paths and King of the Golden River*, Dent, Everyman's Library, London, 1907, p. 120.

5

Social Costs
and Social Change

The concept of 'social costs', as an aspect of economic theory, has been much neglected by economists until recent years. It was first developed by Pigou in 1920.[1] Briefly, the notion of social costs recognises that all the costs of producing a good or service are not borne by the producers, and that all the costs involved in the enjoyment of consumers' goods or services are not borne by the consumers in question. The difference is sometimes described by economists in terms of a divergence between 'private costs' (those incurred directly by the producers or by the consumers of a good) and 'social costs' (those which embrace all the losses and inconveniences inflicted on members of society incidental to the production and enjoyment of a good, in addition to those which enter into the accounts of the consumers and producers).

Joan Robinson put this much more simply when she said that 'one man's consumption may reduce the welfare of others'[2] – a consideration which can be applied to a thousand-and-one forms of individual action – from evading income tax to having large families or owning two houses or organising pop festivals which divert social resources from meeting other needs and thus add to public expenditure.[3]

[1] Pigou, A. C., *The Economics of Welfare*, Macmillan, London, 1920.
[2] Robinson, J., *Economic Philosophy*, Watts, London, 1962, p. 50.
[3] See Department of Health and Social Security, *Public Health Guide Lines for Large Pop Festivals*, August 1971.

One of the classic examples of social costs (cited by Pigou in his book) is taken from an investigation in 1918 by the Manchester Air Pollution Advisory Board into the comparative cost of household washing in Manchester – then a smoky town – as compared with Harrogate – then a clean town. The investigator obtained comparable figures for both towns as to the cost of weekly washing in working-class homes. These showed an extra cost in Manchester of $7\frac{1}{2}$d a week (in 1918) per household for fuel and washing materials. The total loss for the whole of Manchester, taking the extra cost of fuel and washing materials alone, disregarding the extra labour involved on the part of the families, and assuming no greater loss for middle-class than for working-class households (probably a considerable understatement), worked out at over £290,000 a year for a population of 750,000.

In short, these social costs were allowed to lie where they fell and, in relative terms, they fell more heavily on the poorest households. When we look again at this pioneering (but almost forgotten) study we can see that there were three major reasons for this distribution of social costs leading to more social inequality. The first was the difficulty of identifying the causal agents (who specifically was responsible for Manchester being smoky?). The second was the difficulty of allocating compensation to those who suffered the 'disservice' (was it the smoke of Manchester, or a dirty home, or families who did not bother to wash overmuch? In any event, how does one measure on a personal basis the extra costs of extra dirtiness?). The third difficulty was that fifty years ago society did not know how to *prevent* the poverties of pollution and a decaying social environment. Technically, scientifically and administratively it lacked both the knowledge and methods of application even if it had the political will to act. Today we do largely know how to control the quality of the environment and how to prevent the social costs of change from generating poverty and deprivation. We have the scientific, technical and administrative knowledge and skills to act preventively.

This principle of social prevention is thus potentially a critically new component in the concept of social policy. In the past, social policy (like social work) was often seen as simply a process of marginal compensation or mitigation ('picking up the pieces' – like Lloyd George's so-called 'Ambulance Wagon' of National Health Insurance in 1911). Science, technology and the development of administrative skills in Government have now fashioned positive instruments of social policy prevention – if society wishes to use them. But this 'if' in the processes of public opinion raises some fundamental questions of conflicting public choices and values – questions which are relevant to our three Models of Social Policy.

Returning then to the Manchester case study as an example and explanation, we have to recognise that in modern industrialised societies there exists an immense range of social cost elements. They include all direct and indirect losses suffered by third persons or the general public as a result of private economic and social activities – from the costs of collection of litter to the nearly £500 million which road accidents cost in 1970.[1] These social 'disservices' may be reflected in damage to human health; they may find their expression in the destruction or deterioration of property values and the premature depletion of natural wealth; they may also be expressed in an impairment of less tangible values. Considered in relation to all the factors which went into the making of social policy in the past, those which may be described as 'social losses and disservices' were often the most important. H. L. Beales, the social historian of nineteenth-century Britain, said in 1945, in a statement that has often been criticised, that social policy 'is a collective term for the public provisions through which we attack insecurity and correct the debilitating tendencies of our "capitalist" inheritance'.[2]

[1] Dawson, R. F. F., *Current Costs of Road Accidents in Great Britain*, Road Research laboratory, LR 396, 1971.
[2] Beales, H. L., *The Making of Social Policy*, Hobhouse Memorial Trust Lecture, No. 15, Oxford University Press, 1945, p. 7.

In addition to the practical problems of identifying the causal agents and naming those who have been harmed by social costs (like the problems raised by the three million people in Britain aged 16 and over reported by the 1971 Government Survey with some physical, mental or sensory impairment or disability),[1] there is a further difficulty of measuring the time-scale of these effects.

Gurvitch, the French sociologist, has attempted to examine various concepts of time in relation to social class, political ideologies and types of societies. He focuses particularly on the complexity of the temporal. He discusses the error of treating *time* as a unity, when in fact it is multiple. This, he says, is crucial to the sociologist who is involved in attempts to predict and explain. Social roles, attitudes and values move in their own characteristic *time*. They vary in their deviations, in their rhythm, in the degree to which they are dominated by the past, or projected into the future. In his own words, Gurvitch defines '*Social Time*':

'*Social time* is the time of convergency and divergency of movements of the *total social phenomena*, whether the *total social phenomena* are global, group or microsocial and whether or not they are expressed in the social structure. The total social phenomena both produce and are products of social time. They give birth to social time, move and unfold in it. Thus social time cannot be defined without defining the total social phenomenon.'[2]

The concept of social time can also be applied to the institution we call 'social policy'. For instance, *Income Distribution and Social Change*[3] was an attempt to develop, in relation

---

[1] Department of Health and Social Security, *Handicapped and Impaired in Great Britain*, HMSO, 1971.

[2] Gurvitch, G. B., *The Spectrum of Social Time*, Reidel, Holland, 1964, p. 27.

[3] Titmuss, R. M., *Income Distribution and Social Change*, Allen & Unwin, London, 1962.

to needs and dependencies, the notion of 'command-over-resources-through time' (income, wealth and other components of individual 'life chances'). One simple illustration is to consider, in respect of certain functions of the family, different concepts of social time; some families manage their resource allocation in terms of a week; some a month; some a year; some in terms of three generations. At one end of this particular spectrum of social time is the retirement pensioner budgeting from week to week and paying rent from week to week; at the other end are property-endowed families who manage their own resource allocation, through the medium of State-subsidised family trusts (which are tax deductibles), to provide for an unborn third generation – for unborn grandchildren. In short, they spread their resources forward over time extending to durations of up to a hundred years.

Now let us come back to the problem of social costs and the relevance of time and social change. This can perhaps best be illustrated by providing a few concrete illustrations. Towards the end of the 1940s, as a result of scientific and technological advances (or changes) in medicine and allied fields, some maternity hospitals began to administer high oxygen concentrations to certain newly born babies. In 1954, the *Lancet* drew attention to the fact that this 'scientific advance', while benefiting some babies, had caused 'an alarming increase' in the number of babies who, after some months, were found to be otherwise healthy but totally blind.[1] Their expectation of life – and blindness – was approximately seventy years. If they married and had children the effects, social, economic and psychological, could stretch on into the future.

The implications of this form of 'created dependency' (which has little to do with the debilitating effects of capitalism – to refer back to Beales' definition of social policy) for the families involved and for the large range of social services – from income maintenance to social work aid – are too obvious

---

[1] 'Policy for "Prematures"', Editorial, *Lancet*, 2 January 1954, p. 31.

to need underlining. But who were the causal agents and, if they can be identified, for how long – in terms of social time – should they be charged with the social costs of this category of dependency?

The same questions arise, and similar illustrations could be provided, with respect to the consequential or side-effects of the vast expansion in the use, experimentally and otherwise, of new drugs, such as the antibiotics and other diagnostic and therapeutic agents since the 1930s. The disastrous effects of thalidomide in terms of creating generational dependencies provide one dramatic example.

Or consider the increased mechanisation and speed in industrial automated processes and the growing use of ultrasonics, electronics and other techniques in production and distribution. It is estimated that in industrial areas in Britain today up to one-third of all hospital out-patient attendances are attributable to factory accidents. In Britain: 'Every year about 1,000 die as a result of accidents at work. Another half a million people are injured, and 23 million working days are lost every year. The cost of this carnage is almost unquantifiable – some estimates suggest that it ranges from £300 million to £900 million annually.'[1] These are social costs of production which have been transferred – so far as medical care is concerned – to a 'social service'.

Or, again, take the development in recent decades of new chemical processes concerned with the rubber industry, industrial solvents, synthetic detergents, paints and protective coatings, oil refineries, the new plastic industries and so on. We now know – scientific advances making prevention possible – that men employed in the chemical industry are about thirty times more likely than the general population to die of cancer of the bladder. But these are *statistical averages*. For an individual worker the connection between the medical diagnosis of cancer and the nature of his employment and contact

[1] *The Times*, 17 October 1972, summarising a speech by Lord Robens.

with the causal agent may never be made or made too late. The worker, his widow and children will thus have been denied industrial disease benefits and legal compensation.[1]

These are brief and selected illustrations of certain factors of scientific technological change which represent, as disservices, actual or implied threats to the earning power, health and degree of dependency of the individual and his or her family. Dynamic destruction is one of the essential facts about social change – especially economic and technological change. Similar illustrations of a more widespread character could be found in the much larger area of social, political and value changes: the effects of war and other forms of violence, unemployment, enforced idleness (retirement) in old age, rising birth rates, large families and population growth, new public health epidemics as a result of tourism, the spread of credentialism (the ultimate absurdity of which might be that no public gardener would be allowed to grow roses without a Ph.D. in Horticulture), and so on. In all these and other areas of social phenomena – potentially relevant areas for what we call 'social policy' – we have to bring to bear the concept of social time in considering whether these social costs should be allowed to lie where they fall.

Social costs are constantly changing over time. This is one of the effects of social and economic change in modern, industrial societies. As societies increase in wealth with increasing individual wants, the more goods they produce the more goods they need to discard. There is more rubbish to be thrown away, more obsolescence staring us in the face, and more social costs are generated.

Consider the phenomenon of the car in urban societies as one example of the theory that increasing private wealth (among all or part of the population) leads to an increase in social disservices. Here are a few of the social consequences of an increasing consumption of cars which have a bearing on the

[1] Davies, J. M., 'Bladder Tumours in the Electric Cable Industry', *Lancet*, 24 June 1965, p. 143.

provision of public services.[1] More roads are required: new motorways in Britain now cost over £1 million a mile in annual interest charges alone. More houses in the shadow of motorways degenerate into slums with consequential effects on the familes living in them. Motorway borders are becoming the new ghettoes of New York, Los Angeles, Paris and London. More parking space and meters are required. More cars have to be towed away and put to death. There is more diversion of police time to traffic control duties – again, with consequential effects elsewhere. More road accidents leads to a greater demand for ambulances, hospital services, blood transfusion services, disability benefits and so forth. There are more problems of noise, litter and petrol fumes with possible effects on the incidence of lung cancer. There is more need to provide driving test services, standards of road worthiness, lighting services, town planning and, indeed, to reform local government boundaries. The catalogue of social cost chain effects are, indeed, immense.

How should these positive, correcting, preventive, and compensatory services be paid for, and who should be responsible for providing them? They cannot be bought and paid for in the private market by the individual motorist. They cannot be insured against in the private market. There is no monetary profit in the provision of anti-air pollution services, for instance. We set great store by an increase in private wealth – as measured by the consumption of cars – but regard differently (and statistically measure differently) an increase in demand on out-patient, casualty and general practitioner services. Private wealth of this kind is a good, but those things which do not lend themselves to private production, purchase and sale tend, in consequence, to be regarded as a public incubus.

The nature of the fundamental conflict between welfare and economic growth, between economic and social growth is

[1] For others, see Mishan, E. J., *The Costs of Economic Growth*, Staples Press, London, 1967.

currently illustrated by the debate about pollution. As a cause and a protest movement, pollution and conservation have something for everyone. The middle classes and the rich are in favour because they want to protect themselves against the pollutions of airports, the Costa Brava and international tourism. The working classes are in favour because they wish to protect themselves against black immigration, hostels for drug addicts, the homeless, and so on. The radical left are in favour because pollution can be used to implicate multi-national capitalist corporations. And the young are in favour because they see the anti-pollution movement as anti-authoritarian for it is – or so they may argue – resistance to change on the part of the establishment that has resulted in the present situation. So while everyone votes for anti-pollution (just as the Victorians voted against dirt and in favour of a 'sanitary revolution'), no one wants to reduce private consumption or pay higher taxation or employ more civil servants.

Many theories and concepts of social change have been advanced by historians, sociologists, economists and philosophers. Some have sought to explain the present in terms of the past – for example, Marx. Some have developed evolutionary, functionalist and self-equilibrating interpretations of social systems.[1] Boulding sees industrialisation as a continuing process of change and not just as a once-and-for-all 'industrial revolution'. He raises such questions as: what is the meaning of economic progress (or economic growth)? How do we measure economic progress and draw the line between the economic and the social? Does economic progress debauch ends? Does the economic imperative 'Thou shalt get rich' in an age of rising expectations result in societies becoming increasingly ungovernable? He suggests that economic progress (as measured by material and physical criteria) makes a critique

---

[1] An account of these various attempts to explain and analyse change and its consequences is given in Moore, W. E., *Social Change*, Foundations of Modern Sociology series, Prentice Hall, London, 1963. Also relevant is Ch. 2 of Boulding, K. E., *Principles of Economic Policy*, Staples, London, 1968.

of wants all the more necessary, for the better we are able to satisfy our wants the more important it is that our wants should be 'good' wants.[1]

An illustration – and an amusing one – of this particular point is provided by another economist, Galbraith. In his book *The Affluent Society*, he describes an American family going for a picnic in the country

'The family which takes its mauve and cerise air-conditioned, power-steered, and power-braked car out for a tour passes through cities that are badly paved, made hideous by litter, blighted buildings, bill-boards, and posts for wires that should long since have been put underground. They pass on into a countryside that has been rendered largely invisible by commercial art. They picnic on exquisitely packaged food from a portable icebox by a polluted stream and go on to spend the night at a park which is a menace to public health and morals. Just before dozing off on an air-mattress, beneath a nylon tent, amid the stench of decaying refuse, they may reflect vaguely on the curious unevenness of their blessings.'[2]

In a more serious vein, Galbraith suggests, from this illustration, that without collective intervention in the form of positive policies, increasing private wealth can lead to increasing social filth. This principle has also to be seen at work in the urban environment as well as the rural environment. But the causal agents of 'disservice' are generally different. In the rural scene it is primarily the impact on nature of positive external forces. But in the case of the city it is usually the failure to arrest or change, through urban renewal programmes, the processes of decay and obsolescence. This is change – non-beneficent change; for change can be either growth or decay. And it can also simultaneously involve both processes. To

[1] Boulding, K. E., *op, cit.*, p. 23.
[2] Galbraith, J. K., *The Affluent Society*, Hamish Hamilton, London, 1958; Penguin, Harmondsworth, 1970, pp. 196-7.

arrest or change many types of environmental decay is not a process that can be accomplished today by the individual – or by the private market, primarily because the criteria of profitability are not applicable. Marris and Wood argue that the private profit criterion is almost useless today for most of the important decisions in a modern economy;[1] how and where to develop depressed regions and slum districts; how to help the poor; where to site new airports or hostels for the educationally handicapped; whether to aim for more goods or more leisure, and so forth. Consequently, other criteria than the index of profit have to be sought.

But that is not the end of the matter. We cannot consider change – the disservices of change in the form of urban obsolescence and decay – without also considering the effects of these processes on people. It is mainly poor people – disadvantaged people, non-pink as well as pink people – who are exposed to these processes. A number of studies have shown the economic, social, psychological and educational effects of exposure to these 'disservices' of change.[2] Poverty in the broadest sense is implicated – the poverty of feeling, the poverty of the senses, the poverty of language, the poverty of listening and learning, the poverty of social relations – all these poverties may become socially (not genetically) inherited poverties and, according to some students of social conditions, psychologically self-perpetuating poverties.

If social action is to take place in these *personal* situations resulting from 'disservices' then our analysis suggests that it has to come through the discriminating instrumentality we call social policies, social services or welfare programmes.

This problem of urban obsolescence and decay is one example of the many forces of change at work in our societies which are tending to blur the distinction between personal,

[1] Marris, R. and Wood, A., *The Corporate Economy*, Macmillan, London, 1971.

[2] See, for example, Schorr, A., *Slums and Social Insecurity*, Nelson, London, 1964, or Caplovitz, D., *The Poor Pay More*, Free Press of Glencoe, New York, 1963, or Mays, J., *Growing Up in the City*, Liverpool University Press, 1954.

discriminating services and impersonal, nondiscriminating services. We can also see here that one of the causes of blurring and diffusion is the incidence and distribution in the population of the disservices or social costs of change – the costs that discriminate in terms of people.

In his analysis of various theories of change, Wilbert Moore puts forward a number of generalisations under the heading 'The Characteristics of Contemporary Change':

'1. For any given society or culture rapid change occurs frequently or "constantly";
2. Since contemporary change is probable "everywhere" and its consequences may be significant "everywhere", it has a dual basis;
3. The proportion of contemporary change that is either planned or issues from the secondary consequences of deliberate innovations is much higher than in former times;
4. Accordingly, the range of material technology and social strategies is expanding rapidly and its net effect is additive or cumulative despite the relatively rapid obsolescence of some procedures;
5. The normal occurrence of change affects a wider range of individual experience and functional aspects of societies in the modern world – not because such societies are in all respects more "integrated' but because virtually no feature of life is exempt from the expectation or normality of change.'[1]

For our particular purposes, Moore makes three points that are especially relevant. First, the rate of change is accelerating (both in terms of technology and in terms of social values and patterns of behaviour); second, more people are involved; third, the effects may be cumulative. It could be argued from these generalisations that both the advantages (or benefits) of change may be cumulative as well as the disadvantages (or

---

[1] Moore, W. E., *Social Change, op. cit.*, p. 2.

disservices). If this is so, then there are significant implications here in any consideration of the question: 'Is inequality in the broadest sense increasing or diminishing in our societies?' If poverty is self-perpetuating then proportionately more social resources may need to be invested if it is society's will to arrest and change this process. In other words, social policies will have to be more rather than less redistributive in their effects. And they will need to proceed at a proportionately greater rate than the rate of increase in national income or social resources per head of the population.

Looked at in terms of the social, physical and cultural environment – the indiscriminate sector of public services – much the same point may be made. Galbraith suggested that social filth and obsolescence may be increasing at a relatively faster rate than the average increment in the national economic product. He thus argued the possibility 'that the services which must be rendered collectively, although they enter the general scheme of wants after the immediate physical necessities, increase in urgency more than proportionately with increasing wealth. This is more likely if increasing wealth is matched by increasing population and increasing density of population.'[1]

Let us, for the sake of argument, now suppose that society decides that, as well as taking social policy measures to prevent future damages, current and past social costs should not be borne solely by the victims; that some compensation – or welfare service or benefit or legal award – should be provided by someone. But, as yet, neither law nor custom have established an adequate responsibility of the individual producer, consumer or agent for the social or external costs of change. The main body of neo-classical value theory has, it should be remembered, continued to regard such costs as accidental or exceptional cases or as minor disturbances. In some economic textbooks they are described as 'nuisances', which in theory they are. J. A. Schumpeter, the economist, however, saw them

---

[1] Galbraith, J. K., *op. cit.*, p. 106.

as manifestations of creative-destructiveness inherent in all economic and social systems.[1]

What, in general, neo-classical value theory has failed to take into account is that these effects are no longer marginal nuisances – if they ever were. As mentioned earlier in discussing Wilbert Moore's generalisations about social change, the rate of change is increasing; the effects are becoming more widespread and subtle; and increasingly more people are involved. One of the major difficulties – on the supposition that society has decided that the costs should not be allowed to lie where they fall – is that the causal agents are simultaneously becoming more difficult to identify with any precision. Their origins and effects are more multiple and diffused; they manifest themselves in more ways or are seen by society to do so; and they are also being seen as operating in a longer perspective of social time.

The broad implications of the division and diffusion of cause and effect in the whole field of human needs and dependencies are important for social policy. One conclusion we are forced to draw from this analysis is that it is becoming increasingly difficult in modern society to charge the agents, in money terms, with the costs of compensation. We are less able to identify the agents; less able to measure the effects and translate averages into personal needs (social, psychological, generational – as well as economic); and less able to distinguish between those individuals and families who may be thought to justify merit, compensation or redress, and those individuals and families whose claims may be weaker or who may be less able to formulate their claims in a complex society.

In practical action terms, all this is part of the problems of operationally defining need, subsistence and poverty in a world of relativities; the need for education, for new skills, for medical care, for housing, for income maintenance, for social stability, for privacy and so forth. What are the causes

[1] Schumpeter, J. A., *Capitalism, Socialism and Democracy*, Allen & Unwin (4th edition), London, 1954, p. 194.

of need? Why do they exist? Who should be responsible for meeting them? At what standard, and for how long? These are some of the questions presenting themselves to modern societies which have become aware of the existence of needs but which are less certain about the causes which give rise to them.

In Western society, we no longer believe in original Sin; the concept of middle-class guilt has partly taken its place. We no longer believe that disease comes from the gods. We no longer believe in a genetically inferior working class. We no longer believe, or rather most of us no longer believe, that white men are superior to black men. We no longer believe that all the social costs of change should lie where they fall. Poverty, in short, is no longer a crime – as it was in nineteenth-century Britain.

6

Redistribution by the Courts

Should the social costs of change be allowed to lie where they fall – that is, on the individual who has suffered some injustice, and whose life chances are said to have been damaged or destroyed in some form or another even if they cannot be easily measured in material terms? *If* society decides to take any action, the argument shifts from social diagnosis – understanding and generalising about the effects of change – to social action – to formulating and implementing policies which are themselves instruments of positive change to counter the effects of other categories of change.

Two practical questions then are raised for policy-makers. First, who is responsible (individuals or collectivities) for the 'disservices' of change? Can we identify the causal agents in order to charge them with the costs of providing services for those who need compensation and cannot themselves pay for such services? And here there is the problem of distinguishing between the causal agent in general (like smoke pollution) and the specific causal agent (for example the individual owning the chimney or the car exhaust). Second, who should receive the benefits or compensation of such services? Can we, in providing benefits, distinguish between 'faults' in the individual (moral, psychological or social), the legal concept of 'fault' in private accident insurance, and the 'faults' of change? Put concretely, can we say when a coalminer living in a slum house contracts tuberculosis, and needs medical care plus income maintenance for himself and his family, that the mine-owner in the past or the National Coal Board today is responsible, or the landlord of the house, or the man himself or the whole community?

How, for example, should society provide for the man who has been made redundant by automation or whose acquired technical or professional skills have been rendered obsolete by change; for the individual who is capable of and wants to go on working but has been compulsorily retired from work at an arbitrary age in the alleged interests of productivity or in order to promote younger workers and so on; for the worker who is disabled for life in a factory accident?

These are examples of an immense range of 'disservices', social costs and social insecurities which are the product of a changing society and changing values. If these *personal* disservices are not to lie on the individual and his family (which may involve and directly affect three generations – grandparents, parents and children) what redress has the individual? Broadly speaking, industrial societies have sought in the past to find an answer in three different ways. First, individuals have been allowed redress through the law. They are awarded the money value of their damages. Thus Judges have, for instance, to put money value on a particular human life. Second, individuals can insure a 'risk' with a private insurance company in the market (for example, employers' liability insurance, motor and fire insurance, life insurance and so forth). Third, personal discriminating social services and social security services may be provided for all or some part of the population.

For redress through the courts to be successful, the causal agent must be identified and he must be able to pay the damages awarded. For some types of private insurance a similar contingency or uncertainty may operate; the individual who has suffered some loss or damage may not be fully indemnified if, for instance, the employer has not insured a particular risk; if the employer or agent is not found blameworthy; if the insurance company goes bankrupt; if severe inflation reduces the value of the insurance, and so on.

To say that societies have sought to find answers in, broadly, three different ways – redress through the courts of law, insuring 'risks' with private insurance companies and by establishing social services – is, of course, a sweeping generalisation. Every country in the West has developed (and for different social, economic and historical reasons) a different balance of forms of redress, compensation, betterment and redistributive justice.[1]

The United States, for example, relies much more heavily than Britain on the legal system – on redress through the courts. Damages to health, working capacity, length of life and occupational skills (whether caused by industry, accidents, violence, bad medical care or someone else's fault) are generally matters for lawyers, the courts, malpractice insurance and so forth. This reliance on the law has led, among other things, to the growth of 'defensive medical practice' and to increasingly expensive medical and legal systems out of reach of the poorest fifth of American families. Some illustrations of these defensive medical practices are described in *The Gift Relationship*[2] where it was shown that for many people this form of redress through the machinery of the law was increasingly failing to provide answers in a number of critical areas of social policy.

In a different context and for a different risk (or area of need for income maintenance) Britain relies more heavily than the Scandinavian countries on the private insurance market for pensions in old age and for meeting needs brought about by compulsory retirement from work. Again, the historical reasons are different – some of which are explained by Bentley

---

[1] See, for example, Titmuss, R. M., 'Social Security and the Six', *New Society*, 11 November 1971.

[2] Titmuss, R. M., *The Gift Relationship*, Allen & Unwin, London, 1971.

Gilbert.[1] Other reasons may be found in the fact that the private insurance market having been forced, by State intervention, out of the field of disability, sickness and medical care turned its attention to the occupational pension field.

It is interesting, therefore, to examine briefly the classic historical example in Britain of the use of the courts and of private insurance in workmen's compensation. This form of redress epitomises and illustrates many of the problems of identifying the causal agents which, if the private market is to operate and if the cost of disservices are not to lie where they fall, have to be compelled by government to pay monetary compensation for the damage or disservice sustained. We may look for a short time at this example of workmen's compensation. In doing so we should remember that it is also relevant to the discussion of our three models of social policy – and particularly Model A: *the Residual Welfare Model.*

The process we call industrialisation has produced, over the past two hundred years, new risks to life and life chances for the worker and his family. Practically every new industrial development, every new machine and most new technological processes have provoked fresh risks in the form of accidents, poisoning and disease. The social costs, evaluated in terms of death and disablement, in loss of status, skills and earnings for the worker and his family, and in the creation of states of dependency, all involved in industrial advance and rising productivity, have been set down in detail by Wilson and Levy.[2]

In tracing this development we can see the emergence of a fundamental conflict between freedom of contract (as interpreted by nineteenth-century law in the sense of the free and unfettered meeting of wills) and the concept of the family as the basic unit for survival of society. To what extent, if at all, should the State (as expressing the will of the whole community) take any action in this sphere to safeguard the interests

---

[1] Gilbert, B., *British Social Policy, 1919–39*, Batsford, London, 1970.
[2] Wilson, A. T. and Levy, H., *Workmen's Compensation*, Oxford University Press, London, 1939.

of the family? To do so involved a head-on clash with the principles which, enshrined in the law, dominated the relationships between master and man during the nineteenth century.

The legal concept of a 'contract of labour', which grew out of industrialisation and legitimated the private market, meant that the acceptance of wages by a workman implied the acceptance of all risks to life – even if the employee was a child aged 10 in a coalmine or textile factory. To do otherwise would mean, or so it was argued by political theorists and the judiciary in the nineteenth century, that a disguised form of status (the binding together of master and man) would be substituted for the free acceptance of contract. Such a development would have been out of harmony with the growth of economic individualism (resting on individual contract) at a time when society was intent on abolishing status obligations of earlier centuries and loosening the network of social obligations.

Until the Employers Liability Act of 1880, therefore, the injured workman could only obtain compensation by bringing – and winning – a common law action against his employers. To be successful in this he had to prove personal negligence on the part of the employer; but if it could be shown (as it generally was) that the accident was due to the negligence of a fellow-servant then claims were barred by the doctrine of 'common employment'. Legal action by the worker was, moreover, made more difficult by judicial decisions which allowed the defence known as *'volenti non fit injuria'*. This, in effect, meant that the injured workman was said to have known the risks of his employment and to have accepted them – in the mines, factories, ship yards and so on.

Moreover, to be consistent with the theory of the contract of labour it was logical to hold that it was of no concern whatever to the employer whether the injured workman had a wife and children or other relations dependent on him. What, of course, totally and finally abolished this doctrine was the impact of war on social policy. During the First World War not a single voice nor any political party opposed the policy of recognising dependent wives and children when soldiers and sailors were injured or killed. This is but one example of the profound influence that war has exercised on the development of social policy. Once dependency had been recognised in the payment of service allowances and war pensions it was only a short step (though sometimes a delayed one) to similarly recognising the dependants of victims of industrial accidents and unemployment.

When we trace, in this way, the history of this aspect of industrialisation we see that, until the end of the nineteenth century, workmen and their dependants were debarred by law from compensation except in the grossest cases of negligence. Even here, the defence of 'common employment' was invoked to enable employers to avoid responsibility. Indeed, by the middle of the century, the Common Law of England had been so whittled away that in practice it afforded little or no protection to the workman and his family. If social justice was the objective, redress through the courts was seen to be no answer.

In 1897, after decades of bitter conflict, the Workman's Compensation Act was passed. This was, in Britain, the first instalment of what we now call 'social security'. It introduced the principle of 'compensation for personal injury by accident arising out of and in the course of employment'. It represented a combination of compulsory insurance in the private market and redress through the courts.

The Beveridge Report of 1942 analysed the experience of forty-five years of this form of compensation for the social costs and disservices of technological change. Beveridge concluded:

'[This] pioneer system of social security in Britain was *based on a wrong principle* and has been dominated by a wrong outlook. It allows claims to be settled by bargaining between unequal parties, permits payments of socially wasteful lump sums instead of pensions in cases of serious incapacity, places the cost of medical care on the workmen or charity or poor relief, and over part of the field ... it relies on expensive private insurance. ...'[1]

The National Insurance (Industrial Injuries) Act of 1946, which resulted from the Beveridge diagnosis and the Government's subsequent changes in the plan put forward by Beveridge, represented a complete breakaway from the system of workmen's compensation that had existed since 1897. The new system was, according to the Government, to be based on the principles of social insurance. Though called 'insurance' there was to be (unlike Workmen's Compensation) no adjustment to risk, no special incentive to safety (the Beveridge proposal for a levy on hazardous and dangerous trades was not favoured by the Government) and no contribution test for the injured workmen.

Now let us consider some of the basic reasons which justified State intervention in this particular field and an enlargement of the role and functions of social policy. We can apply three criteria to this experience of law and the private insurance market: social justice, social efficacy, and administrative efficiency.

First, let us take the principle that 'Equals in law should be treated equally by the law.'[2] On this principle the law of workmen's compensation failed: this was the conclusion of Wilson and Levy's classic study and of the 1942 Beveridge Report.

Next, take the principle of social efficacy. On applying the test of this principle, the system also failed. It failed to bring about the physical, social and psychological rehabilitation of the injured workmen; this was primarily because it relied on

---

[1] *Social Insurance and Allied Services*, Cmd. 6424, HMSO, 1942, para. 80.
[2] This principle is discussed in Ch. 5 ('Justice and Equality') in Benn, S. I. and Peters, R. S., *Social Principles and the Democratic State*, Allen & Unwin, London, 1961.

monetary compensation alone (often in the form of lump sums) as the answer to the disservices sustained.

Third, let us take the criterion of administrative efficiency – the criterion most often advanced by economists to justify the role of the private market in the field of social policy. It has been shown (in the Beveridge Report and elsewhere) that the administrative costs of private Workmen's Compensation Insurance were of the order of 30 to 40 per cent of the premiums collected. Such figures can now be compared with the administrative costs of the Department of Health and Social Security in administering the present system of National Insurance against Industrial Injuries and Diseases. These costs are in the neighbourhood of 5 to 10 per cent. The private market was many times more costly in terms of administrative efficiency.

Underlying all these reasons for the failure of the private market there was (and is) a deeper and more fundamental one. This brings us back to some of the questions raised in the last chapter. Who is responsible for the disservices and social costs of change? Can we identify the causal agents and can we identify those who should receive special benefits and compensation?

What we have learned historically – in all Western systems as well as in Britain – about industrial accidents and Workmen's Compensation is that the law, based on precedent and case accumulation, has been a failure. It has failed as a form of redress; it has failed to prevent accidents and consequential poverties; it has failed to rehabilitate and re-instate the injured and their families. What it has achieved has been to provide a rich and lucrative market for lawyers and private insurance markets.

Fundamentally, the legal system failed – and is still failing – for two basic reasons. First, because tort liability – that is the legal concept of fault – had as its primary purpose that the role of the law was to make wrongdoers pay for their wrongdoings. Second, and underlying this principle, were the assumptions that wrongdoers could be identified; that all the damages caused over the whole spectrum of social time could be assessed and rewarded in purely monetary forms (for example, the money value of human life, happiness and misery); and that the wrongdoers could, in fact as well as in theory, pay for the damages they had caused.

Evidence for this conclusion that the legal system failed can be derived from a study by Professor Atiyah.[1] After examining accidents and damages in a wide field – car accidents and other forms of damages as well as industrial categories – he shows in detail what is well known to every lawyer, but not often publicly discussed, that the basis of the tort system in awarding damages for 'fault' is more fictitious than real. The amount awarded bears no relation to the degree of fault of the defendant. Many are liable without being at fault in the legal – nor, perhaps, in the moral – sense; and anyway it is practically never the tort-feasor who pays the damages. Moreover, it appears from such unsatisfactory statistics as there are that only about 50 per cent of road accident victims and almost certainly less than 10 per cent of industrial injury victims get any tort damages at all. The remainder have to rely on the national insurance and industrial injuries schemes respectively. These results certainly justify the description of the whole system by another authority, Professor Ison, as a 'forensic lottery'.[2]

It is beyond dispute that the tort system is grossly inefficient and expensive to operate. No more than half the total premium income of the liability insurers ever comes out again in the form of damages paid to accident victims. Professor Atiyah concludes that the case for its abolition is overwhelming.

Tort liability – and the concept of 'fault' in acts of man and and acts of gods – was shaped and developed long before the invention of cars, of machinery, of motorways, of hospitals, of

[1] Atiyah, P. S., *Accidents, Compensation and the Law*, Weidenfeld & Nicolson, London, 1970.
[2] Ison, T., *The Forensic Lottery*, Staples, London, 1967.

penicillin, tranquillisers, tinned and packaged food and holidays, smoke pollution, DDT, hairdryers and virtually all the benefits and costs, the material pleasures and the material nuisances, of science, technology, change, affluence and a mass consumption, Veblenesque conspicuous-consumption society.[1] All changing fashions (in adornment as well as in cars) are Veblenesque; they have to be conspicuous to express change; they impose conforming expenditures (or planned obsolescence) to achieve statuses.

Those who try to understand the meaning and changing roles of social policy have often to seek their materials in strange and seemingly exotic places. A Report in 1970 to Governor Nelson Rockefeller of New York State on automobile insurance[2] begins with a quotation from Kafka's *The Trial*: 'One must lie low, no matter how much it went against the grain.'[3] It then reports that 'In America today, there is no escape from the automobile.'[4] Every day 10,000 people are injured. It is (next to gonorrhoea and syphilis) the most widespread and neglected disease of modern society. During this century more people have been injured by the automobile in the USA than in all the wars that country has been engaged in – the First World War, the Second World War, the Korean War and the Vietnam War.

The report then discusses the mythology of 'fault', the concept of 'wrongdoing', the role of the private insurance market, and all the spiralling, cumulative consequences described as dishonesty, corruption, malpractice, and so forth. It concludes that of all the premiums against 'risks' paid to insurance companies only 14 per cent is ever received by consumers and victims. No action has been taken on this report: to do so would raise questions about social policy and the need for more government and more State bureaucracy. Nor, for

---

[1] Veblen, T., *The Theory of the Leisure Class*, Allen & Unwin, London, 1925.
[2] *Automobile Insurance . . . For Whose Benefit?*, State of New York Insurance Dept., Report to Governor N. Rockefeller, 1970.
[3] *Ibid.*, p. ix.
[4] *Ibid.*, p. 3.

similar reasons, has any action been taken on the report of President Nixon in 1970 on riot and protest insurance in the 'blighted' (or benighted) cities of the USA mentioned in Chapter 1. The major costs of accidents, riots, revolt and violence continue to be allowed to fall on the victims – mainly black people, poor people, old people and handicapped people.

A further strange illustration – though this time somewhat more august and British – is taken from a report from the Law Commission, laid before Parliament by the Lord High Chancellor in November 1970, and called picturesquely, *Civil Liabilities for Dangerous Things and Activities.*[1] It deals with acts of strangers (which may, as a wrongdoing, harm other people); with acts of God (which presumably means unidentifiable as to cause); with dangerous things (which can be left to the reader's imagination); and with escaping things (which covers a far greater range of things than ever went into the Zoo); with public nuisances, private nuisances, and so on. It concludes – without making specific legal recommendations – that the law in all these fields is 'complex, uncertain and inconsistent in principle',[2] and costly.

Many of those who are making these far-reaching indictments of the legal profession are being forced to conclude that over much of the potential social policy area the whole edifice of precedence based on case-law should be abolished. And they are also saying that the adversary procedure (or legal gladiatorial combat) before Tribunals should also disappear.

It is therefore paradoxical in the extreme – as well as disturbing – that, at one and the same time, social workers, academic journalists, claimants' unions and welfare rights people are demanding the introduction of the rigidities of case-law (like Dicey in the nineteenth century who feared both socialism and bureaucracy) and waiting, like Godot, for thousands of lawyers to staff the system as salaried employees paid at about 20 per

[1] *Civil Liabilities for Dangerous Things and Activities*, Law Commission Report No. 32, House of Commons Paper 142, 1970, HMSO.
[2] *Ibid.*, p. 12, para. 20(a).

cent of what they earn in private practice in serving the rich and multinational corporations.

The paradox of enlightened lawyers denouncing the concept of 'fault', case-law, precedence and gladiatorial combat while social workers and others are demanding these procedures and systems is puzzling. Their naïvety may be due to a narrow education, parochial reading and an over-developed sense of professional guilt in relation to their clients.[1]

Accepting, therefore, for the sake of argument that the law has only a very limited role to play in the whole area of social needs, we thus have to consider alternative instruments of social action whose purposes could be concerned with redress, compensation, rehabilitation (in its widest sense) and betterment – in short with redistribution and changing the pattern of the individual's command-over-resources-through-time. In the next chapter we consider how far the principles of insurance can resolve these problems of equity.

[1] See also Titmuss, R. M., 'Welfare Rights: law and discretion', *Political Quarterly*, April, 1971.

7

Redistribution
by Insurance

This chapter is about the theory and practice of redistribution in relation to arrangements for income maintenance – in old age, for widowhood, sickness, unemployment and other risks and situations of dependency. In the public sector of social policy these provisions are generally known in Britain, the USA and other countries as the 'social security system'.

In the privately organised sector of income maintenance, private insurance companies perform the major role. In Britain, as in other countries, these institutions are currently responsible for the organisation and marketing of occupational pension schemes and other so-called fringe benefits for a substantial proportion of the employed male population. Both employer and employee contributions to such schemes are in Britain deductible from taxable income – in whole or in part.

The emphasis on redistribution takes us to the centre of any ideological type of social policy – whether it assumes the character of progressive, regressive, horizontal or vertical redistribution over time. It is thus related to the broader issues of equality and inequality in our societies. Should social policies in the public (and in the private) sectors operate in the direction of more or less inequality in command-over-resources-in-time between different classes and income groups, and in what ways? Should their objective be to lessen existing inequalities; to legitimate and sustain existing inequalities; or to increase them on criteria of merit, work performance, social class and so forth? These questions underlie all past, present and future discussions about the social structure of modern societies.

Social security systems relate to transactions by government (or agencies approved by government) which increase individual money incomes in certain specific circumstances of income loss or need for income protection – for example, old age, widowhood, sickness, disability, unemployment, the dependant needs of children, and so forth. These increments to income may take the form of direct unconditional cash payments or of excusing cash payments by the individual to the government or agency (as in the non-payment of social security contributions during unemployment or sickness – contribution 'credits' – or in the form of deductions from direct taxation). In this context, 'unconditional' means that the payments are not made for specific purposes, such as for the part or full payment of medical bills, drug bills, transport bills, or for the reimbursement of charges for services rendered.

Broadly, therefore, this definition relates to unconditional money income transactions and not to services in kind. It follows the conventional definition of social security (whether described as such in government programmes or as social insurance, national insurance, public assistance, social assistance, national assistance) but includes systems or methods of meeting comparable needs and contingencies through the operations of direct taxation.

By interfering with the pattern of claims set in an economy by the market and by other government actions, social security involves some redistribution in command-over-resources between individuals and groups in society. Whatever the method of finance and the role of contributions, benefits, credits, taxes and tax deductibles the redistributive effects can be classified under two headings: (1) those effects brought about when the system meets *immediate demonstrated need* (for example, public assistance payments); (2) those effects brought about by transactions designed to meet *future pre-*

sumptive need (for example, old-age pension schemes). The distinction is important in understanding the time-span of income distribution or redistribution – past, present and future.

In theory and practice then, every social security system – and there are several hundred different such systems in the world – involves some redistributive effects. But it must not be assumed that 'redistribution' means either 'betterment' or necessarily a lessening of inequality. As mentioned earlier, a substantial part of these transfer payments represents some element of compensation for disservice caused by society – sickness, disability, industrial injuries and accidents, forced retirement from work and so forth. These payments are thus a partial replacement for income loss. Of course, if these compensation payments were not made – if an element of redistribution did not take place – then the range of inequality would be correspondingly increased.

It has been argued that if public social security is seen as an integral part of the modern economy its essential function is the distribution rather than the redistribution of income.[1] Whichever approach is adopted, however, the character and extent of the system's effects will depend on its objectives – modified, as they may be, by the role of taxation. Not all systems, of course, operationally attain their objectives; they may develop unintended or unforeseen redistributive effects as the result of various political, administrative or technical factors. Very few adequate studies have been made, however, of the effective impact of social security programmes on secular changes in the distribution of incomes between groups and classes in society.[2]

If we disregard at this point, however, the difference between theory (objectives) and practice (reality), certain main 'models of redistribution' can be identified which underlie – or are thought to underlie – many income maintenance systems. In a

[1] Merriam, I., 'Overlap of Benefits Under OASI and Other Programs,' *Social Security Bulletin*, US Department of Health, Education and Welfare, Vol. 28, No. 4, April 1965.
[2] For some references to the scanty literature see Gordon, M. S., *The Economics of Welfare Policies*, Columbia University Press, New York, 1963.

world of imperfect competition they are naturally not per-
ceived (nor are they put forward here) as 'perfect models' of
redistribution. They are approximate only and serve merely to
indicate certain major differences in orientation and philosophy.

First, there is (what may be called) the '*individualised actuarial
model*' – a model which forms an integral part of our larger
Model A, *The Residual Welfare Model of Social Policy.* This
actuarial model is the classical, abstract and idealised insurance
model conceptually based on risk theory – individual, collective and general. It results in a contract whereby, for a stipu-
lated consideration, called a premium, one party undertakes to
indemnify or guarantee another against loss by a certain
specified contingency or peril, called a risk, the contract being
set forth in a document called a policy.

Incorporated in this private insurance model are a number
of assumptions: (1) that it is a voluntary contract; (2) that the
individual premium is related to the individual risk; (3) that the
contract will be honoured; (4) that redistribution, in sofar as it
takes place, involves those to whom the contingency occurs and
those to whom it does not. The process of redistribution is not,
therefore, deliberate in the sense that the effects are predictable.

This model of 'drawing-out-what-you-pay-in' (in the language of the common man) has had some influence, ideologi-
cally and semantically, on the shaping of social security systems
in Britain and other countries in the past – particularly those
parts relating to provision for old age. Along with our second
model, it played a political role in the establishment of compulsory social insurance in Germany by Bismarck in the 1880s,
and in the development of National Insurance for unemployment and sickness in Britain in 1911. Technically, it was also
important in Britain in creating the concepts of the 'fund' and
of actuarially determined insurance contributions.

The belief that national insurance did (and should) resemble the private insurance model made it seem inappro-
priate that redistribution from rich to poor should be a
deliberate function of social security systems. The four

assumptions which we have mentioned as underlying this model were thus little questioned in the past. They were automatically taken to be part of the 'natural' functioning of the private insurance market. Consequently, the closer that social security in the past approached this model (before the change in policy to the 'pay-as-you-go' basis), the more effective and politically acceptable it was thought to be.

Yet, when we study the actual behaviour of the private insurance market, it becomes clear that reality hardly ever takes the form of an individualised contract. It is an abstract ideal. What is more relevant is our second model – *'group insurance'*; this is the more appropriate private model to consider in relation to public systems of social security (like, for example, the British 1959 graduated pension scheme).

Incorporated in this model is the widespread belief of many of those covered by group and collective schemes that they have acquired (or have earned or have paid for) an individual contract. Their contributions and those of their employer – conceived as wages or salaries deferred or saved by 'waiting' – *earn* their own benefits; no more, no less. They do not, therefore, see themselves as involved in a system of redistribution. Hence the equally widespread notion which surrounds this model that benefits are 'tailored' to the individual's requirements. He voluntarily chooses his tailored suit, and pays for it himself and with his own contributions and those earmarked by his employer.

Group insurance is the means by which individuals and corporate bodies obtain protection in the private market against one or more of a variety of risks: fire insurance, motor insurance, burglary insurance, life assurance, income reduction in old age and so forth. If admitted to the group they obtain protection as members of a 'contractual sharing group'. The risks are said to be pooled or shared. According to the type of risk the contributions or premiums may or may not be determined by the characteristics of the individual or the property to be covered. More generally today, they are set by the class or category into which the individual or the property concerned is thought to fall – age, sex, occupation, construction and location of property, type of vehicle and its use, and so forth.

The principle of 'pooling risks' is not seen by insurer and insured as *deliberately* redistributive. In practice, of course, the good risks may pay for the bad risks but, on the assumption that the bad risks have been correctly charged higher contributions, there is no intention of redistributing resources from the careful to the negligent property owner, from the good, non-drinking life to the impaired, alcoholic life, and so forth. A good deal turns, therefore, on the extent and quality of risk-rating. If the rating of risks is absent, ineffectual or incorrectly calculated then redistribution will take place as a direct consequence of the assumptions, guesses and methods adopted in price-fixing and the settlement of claims. Thus, an element of deliberate value judgement is interposed – 'deliberate' in the sense of a decision *not* to relate premiums to risk or to do so imperfectly. For example, higher insurance charges may be made on the statistically unsupported belief that certain diseases are inherited; that Jews are poor property risks; that certain employees are accident prone; that working-class households are more negligent than middle-class households; that non-pink people are greater motor-car risks than pink people, and so on.

Developments in mathematical techniques during the past half-century in combination with technological advances in knowledge about risk causation, have all tended to show that actuarial risk- and experience-rating in group insurance is today far from being an exact science. In other words, scientific advances in knowledge have made us more aware of the inexactitudes and imperfections of risk-rating. Insofar as use is consciously not made of these advances in knowledge, the model of group insurance is imperfect – and deliberately more imperfect than, say, fifty years ago – in achieving equity. This, the achievement of equity, is the governing consideration of individual or group insurance – a conclusion reached by an American expert, Mr Reinhard Hohaus:

'Because of its voluntary nature . . . private insurance must be built on principles which assure the greatest practicable degree of equity between the various classes insured. . . . Social insurance, on the other hand, is moulded to society's need for a minimum of protection against one or more of the limited number of recognised social hazards. . . . Hence, just as considerations of equity of benefits form a natural and vital part of operating private insurance, so should considerations of adequacy of benefits control the pattern of social insurance. . . . The foregoing need not necessarily imply that all considerations of equity should be discarded from a social insurance plan; rather the point is that, of the two principles, adequacy is the more essential and less dispensable.'[1]

For private group insurance to strive for the 'greatest practicable degree of equity' means rejecting redistribution as a function of the pooling of risks and reducing to a minimum the extent of accidental or unintended redistribution. This is the theory embodied in the classical model of private group insurance. What today is the reality? How valid are the assumptions stated above in relation to the model?

First, it must be acknowledged that in relation to the Western world in general and Britain in particular remarkably little is known about the bases of modern private risk-rating. It is a large and expanding area of ignorance in which myths abound and facts are scarce; an area virtually unexplored by economists. It is expanding because (and this much is known) the size of 'collectively shared pools' has become much greater with collective price-fixing for large groupings of insurers increasingly substituted for micro-risk rating. In the absence of statistical data we may tentatively submit the following hypotheses concerning the validity of the model. These are not

[1] Hohaus, R. A., *The Record*, American Institute of Actuaries, June 1938, pp. 82–4.

entirely implausible: a certain amount of suggestive information has, for example, been published for many countries in the *Transactions of the International Congresses of Actuaries* during the past twenty years.

1. *That the voluntary nature of the contract is tending to disappear from large areas of private group insurance.*

The last twenty years have witnessed in Europe and North America a great expansion in private insured pension schemes and occupational welfare benefits provided by employers. For the employee, these are generally compulsory whether or not they are contributory and represent wages or salaries deferred on the theory of human depreciation. The employee cannot contract out. He cannot decide to spend his total earnings in alternative ways. Moreover, even if participation is voluntary he has no choice in respect of (a) the cover afforded; (b) the insurer and, generally, there is rarely any formal appeals machinery as there is in some social security systems. Compared with some of these systems, private group insurance may not have a choice of 'best years' of earnings in pension schemes (this is particularly true of manual workers); he may lose some of his rights or expectations if he changes his job; his wife may not benefit if he dies before retirement, and so forth.

In the USA, Father Harbrecht[1] discussed with great learning and scholarship the employees' lack of freedom, and lack of participation in control and security rights under private group pension schemes in that country. In another study, Professor and Mrs Somers concluded in relation to private group health insurance in the USA that 'the consumer is highly limited in his choice'.[2]

---

[1] Harbrecht, P. P., *Pension Funds and Economic Power*, The Twentieth Century Fund, New York, 1959.
[2] Somers, H. and A., *Doctors, Patients and Health Insurance*, Brookings, Washington D.C., 1961, p. 408.

2. *That over large areas of private insurance the individual premium or contribution is increasingly unrelated to the individual risk.*

This hypothesis is in part derived from the trend in modern society for the size of 'collectively shared private pools' to become larger and less subject to conventional market forces. To some extent this is a consequence of the growth in scale of the private insurance market through mergers, take-overs and amalgamations. Prices and policies have become more standardised over larger areas of group insurance; less subject to risk- and experience-rating; possibly more subject to power-rating. Among other factors, what influences the price is less the nature of the individual risk and more the power of financial groups and intermediaries to sell large blocks of insurance business. American experience in the field of private health insurance suggests that '. . . group insurance has become, in large part, a "cost plus" operation . . . some insurance experts now allege that group insurance is no longer really "insurance" in the sense that the carrier assumes the risk but a highly sophisticated form of "insurance" service.'[1] Moreover, price competition is said to be 'almost non-existent'.[2] Some reference to British experience in the pension field in relation to standardisation, the non-competitive aspects of group insurance and risk-rating are to be found in Pilch and Wood's study of pension schemes.[3]

In short, considerations of individual equity are being increasingly sacrificed in favour of considerations of economy of scale in market operations. For instance, medical examinations are rapidly disappearing as a condition of acceptance for privately insured life assurance and fringe benefit schemes in Britain. What is being substituted for the supposed exactitude of individual risk-rating by means of medical examinations is exclusion on certain arbitrary, often untested, criteria, such as

[1] Somers, H. and A., *op. cit.*, pp. 286, 406–8.
[2] *Ibid.*
[3] Pilch, M. and Wood, V., *Pension Scheme Practice*, Hutchinson, London, 1960, pp. 68–74.

absence from employment due to sickness or disability on a specified date; exclusion on grounds of age; exclusion of certain groups, such as unskilled workers, immigrants and women, because they are believed to be subject to a high rate of turnover. They may or may not be 'bad risks': immigrants may not be rejected as immigrants but because they are unskilled, short-term employees; the point is that they are excluded (and thus led to *believe* they are 'bad risks') on grounds of administrative convenience due largely to the growth of large-scale operations.

Equity suffers in the conflict with bigness and those who suffer most are those who fail to fit neatly into predetermined, large-scale classes, categories and groups. Nor is their exclusion from the private insurance market on arbitrary or unsubstantiated risk-rating criteria the end of the matter. Increasingly today, with the spread of private group insurance, it may mean for the individual the denial of work on grounds of age, disability or other considerations and the creation of dependency or, at least, the denial of opportunity of access to certain preferred occupations and careers.[1]

3. *That for substantial numbers of employees covered by private pension and welfare schemes the contract will not be honoured in full.*

When workers change their jobs (for voluntary or enforced reasons) or die in service some part of their accrued pension expectations are lost. Some part of their 'saved' wages disappears. This has been shown by American experience and it is also an increasingly important problem in Britain.[2] Protection under private health insurance schemes and against other

[1] See, for example, Harbrecht, P. P., *op. cit.*

[2] Evidence on this point is given in the report by the Government Actuary, *Occupational Pension Schemes*, HMSO, 1971, and also in Pilch, M. and Wood, V., *op. cit.*, pp. 122–9. The situation in the United States is discussed by M. C. Bernstein, 'Private Pensions in the United States: gambling with retirement security', *Journal of Social Policy*, 1973, Vol. 2, No. 1.

hazards is also lost for similar reasons in the USA and other countries.

Expectations are also eroded by inflation – a process to which the classical model of private group insurance has not yet found an answer in so far as the mass of workers are concerned.[1] Inflation is, as Kenneth Boulding has said 'a refined method of taking bread out of the mouths of the aged, the infirm, the widows and orphans'[2] and feeding it to others be they earners or owners of wealth.

4. *That, contrary to the general belief, private group insurance does have redistributive effects and that these tend, on balance, to be regressive in character.*

The arguments for this hypothesis can be summarised under the following headings:

(a) The absence of risk- and experience-rating. This means, for example, that the true social costs are not borne by the dangerous industries and causative agents – a point stressed earlier. The 'bad risks' are not charged the true market price. Poor workers employed in non-dangerous trades may thus be subsidising higher income groups employed in other trades. The poor, safe driver may be subsidising the rich, bad driver.[3]
(b) The inexact and arbitrary nature of some categories of risk-rating. This allows, for example, more scope for the role of prejudice in price-fixing, in the determination of excluded individuals, groups and classes, and in the settlement of claims. Those who are excluded from standardised schemes may thus be incorrectly charged higher prices for alternative cover or compelled to suffer penalties in other ways.

[1] See, for example, Ratcliff, A. R. and Round, A. E. G., *Transactions of the 17th International Congress of Actuaries*, Vol. III, Part 1, pp. 367–93.
[2] Boulding, K. E., *Principles of Economic Policy*, Staples Press, London, 1959, p. 250.
[3] See, for example, a report by McKinsey & Co., to the British Insurance Association on Motor Insurance, summarised in *The Times*, 10 May 1965.

(c) The practice, in many compulsory pension schemes, of relating benefits to 'final' earnings, which are also maximum earnings for some groups (generally the higher paid classes) but not for other groups (generally the lower paid classes). This practice discriminates against manual workers whose higher earnings in earlier years are not reflected in their pension benefits. This two-type structure of private occupational pension schemes – one type for non-manual and one type for manual workers – may involve some element of regressive redistribution. It is not, we should note, a part of the classical model of private group insurance.

(d) The fact that the costs are reduced or the profits of group schemes are increased by the higher rate of employment turnover experienced by lower-paid workers who (with their wives) lose part or all of their pension and other welfare expectations.

As a relatively higher proportion of manual workers (compared with non-manual workers) do not, on changing jobs, receive back what they and their employers have paid in, the result is a substantial element of redistribution from lower-paid workers to higher-paid workers.

(e) The likelihood that a disproportionate share of the administrative costs of group schemes may be loaded on certain classes of insurance. This is conjectural but some historical evidence is suggestive.[1] In some cases, these classes of insurance cater predominantly for lower-paid workers – as, for example, workmen's compensation insurance in a number of countries.

(f) The fact that in Britain and other countries the private insurance market has exacted substantial concessions from the fiscal system and that these concessions favour the higher income groups.[2] The 'impact effect' of these concessions is borne by the whole population.

---

[1] See *Social Insurance and Allied Services*, Appendix D, Cmnd. 6424, 1942.

[2] See, for example, Lynes, T. A., 'Life Assurance through Pension Schemes' (Appendix D), in Titmuss, R. M., *Income Distribution and Social Change*, Allen & Unwin, London, 1962.

(g) The fact that in an inflationary economy the 'impact effect' of employers' contributions for private group schemes is generally borne by the purchasers of the firms' products – in effect, the whole population of non-earners as well as earners – and may be regressive in character.[1]

(h) The fact that *average* mortality tables are applied indiscriminately to rich and poor alike over large areas of private group schemes. As it is now known that the higher income groups have a longer expectation of life than the lower income groups, the result is on balance redistribution in favour of the former – particularly when account is taken of the effects of tax deductibles for contributions, premiums, lump sums, loan charges and other factors.

A study published in 1965 by the Institute of Actuaries on the mortality of pensions under private group pension schemes contains some interesting material. It shows a considerable excess mortality among those insured under schemes for manual workers compared with the rates for non-manual workers. The report concluded: '. . . it is apparent that the higher paid pensioners have a lighter experience and that class differences in mortality extend into old age. This finding has important implications for the conduct of pension scheme business. . . .'[2] In short, it would seem that the poor pay more in the private market because they are poor and because they are statistically treated as non-poor.

These attempts to examine the validity in practice of the classical (or should we say 'conventional'?) model of individual and group insurance in the private market can now be summarised. We have considered four major hypotheses relating to:

1. The voluntary (freedom of consumer choice) element – or assumption.

[1] See, for example, Gordon, M. S., *The Economics of Welfare Policies*, Columbia University Press, 1963.

[2] *Transactions of the Faculty of Actuaries*, No. 220, 1965, pp. 8, 18, 20.

2. The equity assumption: that individuals are subject to risk-and experience-rating, and that they do pay the 'true market rate'.

3. The assumption that all contracts will be honoured in full.

4. The assumption that no element of redistribution from income group to income group or from class to class is deliberately built into these private pension schemes.

In looking at what is known in practice (as distinct from economic and actuarial theory) we have to say that there is little evidence to support these four hypotheses. We must not, of course, conclude that this particular analysis wholly disposes of the case for or against these private market institutions. There are other considerations of a non-social policy nature which should be brought into account. But from the partial approach of social policy considerations there would seem to be little substance in these four hypotheses.

Finally, two general conclusions can be drawn from this exercise which have a bearing on our three models relating to the role of social policy.

First, it is now widely accepted that in all sectors of the economy there is a national need to diminish both the absolute fact and the psychological sense of social and economic discrimination. This aim, it has been argued, should be applied to the problems of status discrimination between manual and non-manual workers; discrimination on grounds of age, sex and marital status; discrimination against those who have to change their jobs, learn new skills, move to other parts of the country, retire from work earlier or experience unemployment in the interests of economic growth; discrimination between pink and non-pink people, and so on.

By its nature it seems that the private insurance market cannot fully meet this national need. On the contrary, as our analysis indicates, recent tendencies are in the other direction: towards hardening differentials and enlarging areas of felt discrimination.

Second, in Britain, as in other countries, it is increasingly argued that one of the aims of social policy should be 'to concentrate help on those whose need is greatest' and to enable these groups in the population 'to share in rising national prosperity'. This was the basis of the American and Canadian 'Wars on Poverty' – campaigns that have been heavily influenced by the public recognition of (a) the human consequences of automation and cybernation, (b) the threat of increasing violence from those who are excluded from society on economic, social and civil rights grounds.

Again, in the field of income maintenance and social security provisions generally, the private insurance market has voluntarily made little contribution towards the attainment of these national objectives. This is understandable, logical, and consistent because of the fundamental differences between the concepts of social security and 'insurance' and their distributive justice objectives. One is mainly concerned with meeting needs; the other rests on quite different criteria.

8

British Pension Plans – a case study

In the last chapter we examined the role, function and objectives of private insurance and public social security. In this chapter we apply these themes to pensions for widowhood and old age by examining two alternative pension plans for Britain, one proposed by the Labour Government in 1968 and the second proposed by the Conservative Government in 1971. These two contrasting schemes illustrate how different value systems can result in complex redistributive consequences which are not always apparent at first sight nor made explicit by those who present the proposals.

This is a topical issue in Britain. It has been topical since the Labour Government's much criticised National Superannuation Bill was first made public and ultimately consigned to history after the election of 1970. It has been made even more topical by the Conservative Government's recasting of Social Security by the Social Security Bill of 1973[1] foreshadowed in the White Paper *Strategy for Pensions*[2] published in 1971. It has also been made topical by the entry of Britain to the Common Market.

It is only when one adopts a comparative approach and analysis that one can distinguish something of the nature of the real choices and priorities in social policy – which, in the

---

[1] It was still a bill at the time of Titmuss' death (eds).

[2] Department of Health and Social Security, *Strategy for Pensions*, Cmnd. 4755, HMSO, 1971.

ultimate, is all about the dilemmas of choice and change, individual liberty and collective responsibility. To make such a comparison between the Conservative Government's scheme and the Labour Government's National Superannuation Bill 1970 will show that choice in this particular area of social policy is not just a matter of detail – of marginal differences in administrative organisation and social engineering. At bottom, the real choice consists of two fundamental contrasting views of the objectives of social policy and different interpretations of the nature of man.

In industrialised societies today – Britain, Sweden, the Soviet Union, the Common Market countries and so on – no new pension plan can start with an entirely clean slate. Decades of accumulated rights, contributions, expectations, anomalies and inequities are inherited. They cannot be corrected overnight but they can be resolved over time; thus two of the issues are: how quickly and for whom?

The Labour Government inherited in 1964 a greater pension muddle of anomalies and injustices than that existing at the time in many industrialised societies. It was that muddle also, accentuated by the passage of time and other factors, with which the 1971 White Paper attempted to come to grips.

Before, however, we come to 1971 let us look briefly at the major structural changes envisaged in the 1970 Bill. First, in breaking away completely from the flat-rate principles of Beveridge (called National Insurance) it set out a comprehensive scheme of earnings-related social security based on the objective of adequacy – an adequate income for future pensioners who had no other means. Adequacy was defined in terms of a guaranteed income in retirement for an average earner and his wife of between 50 to 65 per cent of their combined pre-retirement life earnings. Because of the effects of the redistributive formula built into the scheme, the low wage-earner would receive a higher proportion. These benefits were not only to be inflation-proofed during the 'build up' through working life for both men and women and linked to the cost of living after retirement – thus guaranteeing adequacy – but also to be 'dynamised' to keep pace with economic growth.

A second objective, closely related to the first, was to prevent future poverty in old age and to reduce the number of pensioners needing to apply for means-tested Supplementary Benefits. Hence, the Bill proposed that everyone should be 'blanketed-in' in a twenty-year build-up. That is to say, instead of having to wait for forty-seven years (for male new entrants at age 18) – the period for which people would have had to contribute in strict actuarial terms – full 'dynamised' pensions would be paid within twenty years. This meant that all those currently over the age of 40 would be heavily subsidised – a redistributive effect particularly favouring married women re-entering the labour market and older immigrants from Commonwealth countries. And it also meant, as *The Economist* pointed out, 'this generation solemnly voting itself bigger pensions requiring substantially bigger contributions to be paid by our children than we have been prepared to contribute towards our parents' and grandparents' pensions now'.[1] *The Economist*, therefore, came down on the side of children and young people today (as the new White Paper has also done) in arguing that they should not be irrevocably committed to make larger sacrifices in their working life to support – through State compulsion – their parents and other people's parents in old age.

This twenty-year 'blanketing-in' (plus the dynamic provision to adjust pensions for economic growth) in the National Superannuation Bill was more generous (and entailed more sacrifices to aid 'stranger' parents and grandparents in the future) than any other social security system in the world. Even in Sweden, the far-reaching pension reforms of the 1960s only legislated for a thirty-year period of 'blanketing-in'.

The logical consequence of these 'blanketing-in' proposals, of the redistributive formula favouring the lower paid, of

[1] *The Economist*, 18 September 1971.

dynamised credit awards during periods of unemployment, sickness and so forth, meant, in effect, the complete overthrow of strict actuarial principles, of risk-rating individuals and groups, of the concept that no man or woman should subsidise the pensions of other men and women. Thus, the scheme was financially to be run on a 'pay-as-you-go' basis. Behind this was the philosophy that only by State action could each generation be compelled to redefine 'adequacy' and 'relative poverty' in terms of the average standards of life enjoyed by future generations.

The main principles and the general direction of change embedded in what was an immensely complicated social security Bill can be summarised under five headings:

1. *Redistribution*

In overthrowing the actuary and the principle that each individual should buy only his own security, the Bill incorporated a variety of redistributive mechanisms favouring low-wage earners, older generations between 40 and 65, older immigrants and contributors, people experiencing prolonged periods of sickness, disability and unemployment, and women. In particular, and compared with the pension situation as it was in 1970, the Bill represented an entirely new deal for women; it shifted more resources and more legal rights to social security in favour of women – married, single, divorced, separated and widowed. It took into account – and dynamised – all their contributions in work at any age, however many interruptions there were because of marriage, childbirth, child care and retraining. It also gave them a new set of legal rights to take over or inherit ex-husbands' and deceased husbands' dynamised contribution and credit records both before the first marriage as well as during the marriage. As a charter for married women, widows and ex-wives it went further than any other social security system in the world.

2. *From subsistence to adequate pensions*

The Bill marked a transition from the concept of minimum or subsistence income maintenance (enshrined in the Beveridge Plan and embodied in National Insurance with benefits below Supplementary Benefits standards) to the concept of adequacy.

3. *A guaranteed redefinition of adequacy*

By adopting various mechanisms of dynamisation, the Bill incorporated a commitment by society to a continual process of redefining adequacy in relation to rising standards of living. It thus presumed a willingness by society to accept an enlarged role for collective altruism in the future. In effect, it committed future generations of contributors to the prevention of poverty and to reducing the role of means-tested Supplementary Benefits.

4. *Earnings-related contributions and benefits*

By introducing, for both men and women, some degree of relationship between social security benefits and revalued earnings throughout working life (in place of the flat-rate system), the Bill narrowed the disparities between manual workers (peak earnings in early life) and non-manual workers (peak earnings just before retirement). Again, this benefited the great proportion of working women. Moreover, the fact that compulsory earnings contributions by employees were limited to one and a half times average industrial earnings (dynamised) whereas there was no ceiling at all for employers introduced a further substantial redistributive mechanism.

5. *The role of social security in a more 'open' and 'fluid' society*

In economic and social terms, many of the detailed proposals in the Bill recognised that, looking to the future, it is reasonable to expect: more job-changing and more occupational and geographical mobility among both men and women at all ages; more emphasis on retraining and further education throughout life; less rigidity in the labour market, resulting in more changing of occupational careers; more people in part-time work offering more diversities of interest, freedom and challenge among both sexes at various periods in working life (especially among women); and probably more frequent and more widespread periods of 'resting between engagements' (due to enforced or voluntary unemployment, training and retraining, or a need to care for children and old people).

Such trends towards a more fluid and adaptable society pose immensely complicated problems for all State social security systems (within and without the Common Market) and particularly for the 65,000 separate and different occupational pension schemes. They raise questions of equivalence of benefits, preservation, transferability and the inheritance of contributions, and the role of credited (or notional) contributions during periods of non-working.

The Bill looked to the future in the sense that many of its complex provisions were designed to accommodate and facilitate such changes in society. They had to be complex because of the muddles of the past and in order to simplify life for people in the future. Simplification for the consumer in our social arrangements is – we should remember – an important element in freedom for many people who do not and cannot afford to employ lawyers (who anyway are seldom interested in poor clients) and tax consultants and accountants (who rarely provide services in CABs and Information Centres).

None of these five objectives I have summarised was attainable without a universal, compulsory, contributory State system geared to the objective of dynamised adequate income support. Thus, the role of the State had to be dominant in the whole structure of income maintenance in old age and other situations of economic dependency.

The Bill recognised and accorded a complementary or subsidiary role for occupational pensions (private and public) on top of the State scheme. But, given the realities of the situation and the high standards of equivalence set for con-tracting-out, the private market role would, in the future, decline to the status of a junior partner – and then mainly for the upper- and middle-income groups. In effect, therefore, the National Superannuation Bill radically reversed the trends of the 1950s and 1960s towards a more dominant role for the private market.

So much then for the main design of a Bill which, after the election of June 1970, was politically banished to the archives of the Public Record Office for study by future historians of social policy.

The main proposals of the Conservative Government[1] are set out most clearly in the White Paper, *Strategy for Pensions*. They can be examined in terms of contrasting principles. They are separately considered in three sectors: the State Basic Scheme, Occupational Pensions and the new State Reserve Scheme.

The State Basic Scheme

This resurrects and maintains the principle of subsistence or minimum flat-rate pensions for all. Indeed, the White Paper goes further because in paragraph 13 it is made clear that basic pension benefits must continue to be 'poverty pensions'; that is to say the benefits must continue to be about £2 per week below the Supplementary Benefit or 'poverty line' in Britain. Thus, there is to be no respite for the Supplementary Benefits Commission; on the contrary, and for reasons ex-plained later, we must expect an increasing number of people to receive 'selective' means-tested pension benefits.

For these 'poverty standard' pensions the contributory principle in National Insurance is overthrown in reality though not in name. What is to be substituted for employees is a compulsory direct tax (though unlike taxation disregarding circumstances) up to one and a half times (or currently about

---

[1] A Conservative Administration took office following the election of June 1970.

£60 per week) of average male industrial earnings. Employers will pay the same; thus, there will not be the element of redistribution from employers that there was in the National Superannuation Bill (which would have required employers to pay a percentage contribution on their total pay-roll).

These taxes on employees will have to be paid for forty-four years (men) and thirty-nine years (women) if full entitlement to a poverty pension is to be secured. Those who pay taxes for shorter periods will get lower poverty pensions. There is provision for crediting contributions during periods of unemployment, sickness, disability and approved training. But these credits are set at the lowest possible minimum (currently £9 per week) whereas the National Superannuation scheme envisaged a much higher value for credits plus dynamisation. In effect, therefore, late entrants (like immigrants) and those experiencing the most unemployment and sickness will be heavily penalised for the 'diswelfares' of society; the costs of such 'diswelfares' will, in the main, lie where they fall. Inevitably, therefore, they will all in the future be claimants for means-tested supplementary benefits.

Unlike the National Superannuation Bill, there is to be no inflation-proofing of the tax-contribution. All that is promised is a biennial (or annual) review of pensions in payment. With rising standards of living, therefore, the gap will widen between the value of poverty pensions and average earnings in real terms.

Married women in the Basic Scheme are treated as dependants of their husbands, and are so described. They must not, therefore, be compelled, if they work, to pay the tax or contribution. Instead, they are to be offered freedom of choice to pay a direct tax.[1] If they do pay they will, in effect as dependants, receive little benefit from so doing. This is about the most flagrant piece of dishonesty about 'freedom of choice' perpetrated on women in any social security scheme.

[1] *Strategy for Pensions*, para. 47.

Occupational Pensions

The major strategy of the Government is greatly to enlarge the private market sector of occupational pensions – either through insurance companies or by firms setting up self-assured schemes. Thus, one of the main objectives of policy is 'to give every employee the opportunity to build, on the foundation of the Basic Scheme, an earnings-related pension scheme, or failing that a State Reserve Scheme'.[1]

According to the last survey of occupational schemes by the Government Actuary, it was estimated that about 62 per cent of all male workers and 28 per cent of female workers had some occupational pension cover at the end of 1971.[2] But this was only an estimate, as 33 per cent of all the firms approached to complete a simple questionnaire failed to respond. It was also estimated that there were some 65,000 different and independent occupational schemes each with their own rules, regulations, benefit structures, and so forth. They will all need revising and changing when the new legislation comes into effect.

Of the total of some 11·1 million people in pension schemes in 1971, 4·1 million were in the public sector (the National Health Service, the Civil Service, local government and the nationalised industries). In the private sector, with 7 million members, a much lower proportion of all employees were covered. At the most, it would seem that the following proportions of workers in the private sector had some expectation of some occupational pension:

	%
Non-manual employees (male)	75
„ „ „ (female)	36
Manual employees (male)	45
„ „ (female)	19

Clearly, the two groups who have benefited least from the

---

[1] *Ibid.*, para 8.
[2] *Occupational Pension Schemes, 1971*, HMSO, 1972, p. 5.

development of occupational schemes are women (of a total labour force in Britain in 1971 of nearly 21 million over 7 million were women) and manual workers (representing over 53 per cent of the labour force).

But these figures of coverage really tell us very little about the nature of these schemes and their ultimate value to the members of such schemes. The questions one needs to ask about them – particularly in the private sector – include:

1. The value of the pension on retirement in relation to lifetime earnings (and not just pre-retirement earnings) and the extent to which account is taken of inflation during the whole of working life.

2. Whether and to what extent pensions in payment are subsequently increased to take account of inflation.

3. Whether and to what extent benefits are paid for widows, widowers and other dependants during service and/or in retirement.

4. The effects of excluding certain categories (such as the sick, the disabled, strikers, part-time workers, older workers, women re-entering the labour market after age 40, immigrants on work permits, and other actuarial 'bad risks') and the effects of limiting age at entry (particularly among women and manual workers) to age 25 or 30.

5. The effects of job-changing labour turnover taking into account non-preservation or only partial preservation of pension rights particularly among manual workers and women aged under 30.

6. With more divorce, separation and re-marriage what provision is made for an equitable allocation of 'earned pension rights' and savings between those involved in more than one marital partnership. This question raises the whole issue of property rights, inheritance, legal maintenance and so forth between men and women.

7. The effects of bankruptcies and mergers among insurance companies and private enterprise firms and the problems raised when self-assured schemes invest their funds in the firms' business. Who then controls the firm?[1]

The whole area of private pension schemes – and occupational welfare in general – is an area of almost total statistical blackness surrounded by barriers of silence.

If there is a general lack of knowledge about pension schemes it would seem to follow that millions of those who are members or ex-members of such schemes know little about their rights, benefits and expectations. Nor is there any formal appeal system. An increasing number of people as they change their jobs, experience unemployment, get married and separate, will be collecting on retirement many little bits and pieces of partially preserved or 'frozen' pension rights, most of them having dwindled further in value as a result of inflation. The problem of keeping track of all these bits and seeing that they are in fact paid when they should be paid could well turn out to be an 'administrative nightmare' for the private pension sector.

But, apart from all these issues and the absence of hard facts, it is clear that 'adequate occupational cover for everyone is not ... in sight'.[2] Benefits are 'meagre' under some schemes 'even after many years of service'[3] and provision for manual workers, women and widows is inadequate or totally non-existent.

It is therefore proposed greatly to stimulate the growth and development of occupational schemes by tax subsidies and in other ways so that the occupational pension sector comes to dominate the area of income maintenance in old age and widowhood. A supervisory Occupational Pension Board is to be set up to lay down certain minimum conditions which will have to be met by employers in order to obtain exemption from paying contributions to the Reserve Scheme.

[1] On this issue, see Harbrecht, P. P., *Pension Funds and Economic Power*, The Twentieth Century Fund, New York, 1959.
[2] *Strategy for Pensions*, para. 26.
[3] *Ibid.*, para. 25.

The main conditions are:

1. The scheme must provide a personal pension for men at an annual rate of not less than 1 per cent of earnings. For women, the minimum is set at 0·7 per cent to take account of their average greater longevity.

2. A widow's benefit (after retirement) representing half the husband's pension rate must be provided. In the case of death in service a lump sum can be paid (again, nothing is said about how such lump sums are to be divided between wives, ex-wives and other dependants).

3. Schemes will not be required to protect the value of contributions during the 'build-up' of rights during working life. Those starting work after leaving school and manual workers with peak earnings earlier in working life will thus suffer particularly from the effects of inflation. With inflation at a rate of, say, 5 per cent a year their pensions will be derisory when they reach retirement age. For non-manual workers, however, who reach their peak earnings just before retirement there will be a high degree of 'inflation proofing', particularly as there are apparently, to be no *maximum* conditions laid down (apart from those set by the Inland Revenue). The effect of all this, given even a moderate degree of inflation in the future, will be highly redistributive in favour of non-manual workers, professional people and all those in the top salary bands.

4. The Scheme will be required to protect the value of the pension after award, generally by linking it to the cost of living index. But the condition will be of little benefit to those whose pensions are worth very little on retirement. And, incidentally, the administrative costs of the re-valuing every year of two millions of small pensions worth, perhaps, 50p to £1, and carried by some 65,000 different occupational schemes, will involve immense computer and administrative costs as well as a great increase in private data banks.

5. Approved and exempt schemes will have to preserve pension rights and pay out at retirement age the bits and pieces of 'frozen pensions' (no account is to be taken of changes in the value of money). These 'frozen bits' will then presumably have to be continually re-valued according to post-retirement changes in the cost of living (another administrative nightmare for private schemes).

But, in order to reduce the volume of work somewhat, no one will be entitled to a preserved pension unless he or she has stayed in the same job for five years *and* attained the age of 26 before leaving. All those who leave school at 16 and work for 10 years (men and women) will be denied the opportunity of receiving a frozen pension. Moreover, many workers and low-wage earners who change their employers frequently – or who are forced to do so by unemployment, sickness, industrial mergers and bankruptcies – may never receive any frozen pensions whatever their age. In addition, the freedom of choice (especially important to women who leave their jobs on marriage or the birth of a baby) of allowing workers to get a cash refund of contributions after some years of service under or over the age of 26 is to be withdrawn. This is a concrete example of the principle that more freedom for the rich in the private sector means less freedom for the poor.

Of course, the logic of these proposals is that no young people, women or low-wage earners should change their jobs within a period of five years – if that, in practice, were possible, particularly in those areas of the country now experiencing high unemployment rates. Many economists would point out that such a degree of immobility and rigidity in the market for unskilled women, young people, single and married women would have highly undesirable effects on the economy. However that may be, the promotion of occupational pensions and their preservation on these conditions *may* introduce and lead to more occupational mobility among skilled manual and non-manual workers, the middle classes and professional staff.

The cost of this freedom of job-changing, however, will be paid for either in terms of less mobility among the unskilled, low-wage earners and women or lower pensions for these groups in old age.

One conclusion which can be drawn from this brief description of the new legislation, and after comparing it with the National Superannuation Bill, is that looked at as a whole it represents a major instrument for the enlargement of inequalities in old age, between men and women and between low-wage earners and those on or above average wages and salaries. This conclusion is endorsed when one examines the structure of the State Reserve Scheme.

The State Reserve Scheme

As mentioned earlier, the White Paper acknowledged that occupational pension cover for everyone 'is not in sight'. Therefore, there must be on top of the Basic 'poverty' pension a 'fall-back' or Reserve Scheme. But – and this is crucial – the Scheme must not 'rival' the private sector; it must be 'modest' – like all reserve teams it must be made to be inferior to the private sector and must be regarded as inferior, otherwise employers will shift their responsibilities for pension onto the taxpayer. In this context then, 'selectivity' means not concentrating resources on those whose needs are greatest but selectively and deliberately providing inferior pension for such groups.

The Scheme is designed on an actuarial and commercial basis. There is to be no contribution or subsidy from the Exchequer and (unlike private schemes) employees' contributions (set at 1·5 per cent of earnings) will not be tax-deductible (one example of discrimination in favour of the private sector). Everyone in the Scheme (or in and out of the Scheme) will take out according to what they (and their employers) actually pay in in money terms – no more, no less. It is thus modelled on individualistic, actuarial criteria. No one will be allowed to join the Reserves until they are age 21 (this, of course, ignores the work contribution between the ages of 16 and 21). To obtain a full 'modest' pension, therefore, at age 65 (men) and 60 (women) contributions will have to be paid for forty-four years continuously (men) and thirty-nine years (women).

During periods of unemployment, sickness, disability, industrial injuries, maternity and so forth no credited contributions at all will be awarded. This is actuarial theory at its purest, not matched by so-called actuarial occupational schemes for middle- and higher-income earners who continue to receive their salaries (and pension contributions) when they are away sick or get maternity leave or receive paid sabbaticals or are sent on training schemes. This is another example of discrimination against the unskilled, the low-wage earners experiencing chronic sickness, and those who are most exposed to periods of unemployment and most need re-training and rehabilitation. It could operate as a disincentive to re-training and rehabilitation – particularly for those in their fifties who will reduce their pension entitlements if they undergo such courses instead of continuing in an unskilled job.

The Scheme is to be fully funded – like commercial schemes – and run by an 'independent Board of Management'. It must invest its funds in equities and property – the funds compulsorily derived in the main from the poorest third of the total labour force in Britain. But there is to be no 'back-door' nationalisation. The Board will not be allowed to purchase more than 5–10 per cent of the equity shares of any one firm (which is hardly consistent with commercial criteria).

If the Board makes a profit, bonuses will be added to pensions in payment and to the prospective pensions of those who have not yet reached pension age. If it does not – and there is no guarantee that it will – members of the Reserve Scheme will have no protection at all against rising prices.

Who will these members be? A 'highly conjectural' estimate by the Government Actuary suggests that at the start there might be 7 million members. It is thought that about half of them will be women, single, married, unmarried mothers, separated and deserted wives. The rest will be made up of low-wage earners, the intermittently employed, men aged 21 to 26, those employed by small firms, agricultural workers, quite a lot of black people, citizens of the Republic of Eire, ex-prisoners, ex-mental hospital patients, new immigrants on work permits and many others who are not regularly employed through life by one or two employers. It is, in a sentence, a Reserve and inferior scheme for women, the 'under class' and all the 'bad industrial risks' in our society. There is nothing like it in all the Common Market countries. 'Social security harmonization' becomes little more than a fantasy. Paradoxically, it is the most anti-Common Market scheme that could theoretically have been devised.

Given these three sectors of pension provision, the Basic Scheme, Occupational Pensions and the Reserve Scheme, there is no prospect in the foreseeable future of reducing the number of old people in receipt of means-tested Supplementary Pensions. The fundamental ideological long-term objective – and it is more long-term than short-term because of the inheritance from the past – is Model A of Social Policy, the Residual Welfare Model in which a dominant role is played by private market institutions. Only a minor role is allotted to Government – to collective social policies – and then only in respect of a minority of strangers, those with below average earnings, the residual labour force and the public assistance sector. In the shorter term, Britain will have, in effect, a four-tier structure of income maintenance systems in old age.

First, at the top will be occupational pensions based on the individualistic principle of 'drawing-out what you pay in'. It is thus achievement-oriented, focused primarily on men and regarding wives as dependants, and assumes regular and stable employment and career patterns after the age of 26. In concept and theory it is non-redistributive; it simply rewards achievement and compulsory deferred consumption (or compulsory savings) throughout working life. In practice, however, it will be heavily redistributive in favour of the higher income groups, (a) because of the greatly increased subsidies to such schemes through the tax system, and (b) because the deficiencies of the private market schemes (such as non-preservation at certain ages, irregular employment, immobility of labour, the low earning sector and others mentioned earlier) will be transferred to and picked up by either the Reserve Scheme or the Supplementary Benefits Commission in combination with the universal basic poverty pensions.

Second, there will be basic pensions which for a time will under-pin the growth of occupational pensions. But primarily they remain because of past commitments and the need to provide for the present generation of old people. However, they are not to be allowed to grow and are to remain fixed at below subsistence standards. Over time, they seem likely to be phased out as more people receive occupational pensions. The insurance principle is overthrown (it can safely be discarded now with the renaissance of actuarial principles in occupational pensions and the Reserve Scheme). One could describe it as subsistence universalism, flanked by selectivity favouring the upper income group and selectivity disfavouring the poor.

Third, there will be the State Reserve Scheme which is designed to make the private occupational sector superior, more attractive and more efficient. Hence, it must deliberately be made inferior and it must pick up – on a commercial basis – some of the casualties and diswelfares in modern society, and some of the defects in the occupational pensions sector.

Finally, and at the bottom of the hierarchy there will be the Supplementary Benefits Sector – the means-tested sector – the repository of all the consciences of society and the guilts of the middle classes who at one and the same time dislike stigma, but indulge in the process of stigmatisation. In the future, it seems likely to grow in scale – and thus it will involve more progressive redistribution as it is at present wholly financed by the taxpayer.

The whole strategy of the Conservative Government looked to the past, to the myths and nostalgias of the nineteenth century; to a man's past, dominated by the virtues of individualism, actuarialism, risk-rating, saving, achievement and the order of regular stable career patterns ending in peak earnings before the relaxations of retirement; to a world in which you only gave to strangers through charity or the poor law.

In comparative terms, the National Superannuation Bill was revolutionary not only in its redistributive effects or in the enlarged role it envisaged for 'Gift Relationships', but in the way it looked forward rather than backwards. It gave a new deal to women. It recognised a future in which there would be more needs and demands for a more open and mobile society; in which the roles of men, women, marriage and the family would change; in which science, technology and commonsense would require more people to be free to change their jobs, be re-educated, re-trained and rehabilitated. Above all, it recognised the need for people to know their rights. The essence of 'rights' in non-means-tested pension and social security systems is not just to know that you have a 'right' to a pension. It is to know that you are entitled to claim a precise predetermined sum; to know what precisely you may expect by way of income under certain circumstances and at a stated age.

Under the new scheme large numbers of people will not know, in this sense, their expectations. As they – both men and women – move through life, from one occupational scheme to another, in-and-out of the Reserve Scheme, from half-time work to full-time work and vice versa, from work to family and re-education and back to work, from marriage to divorce or desertion or widowhood and re-marriage, from work to unemployment and sickness and back again to work, they will be accumulating, Kafka-like, bits and pieces of preserved and frozen claims, fragments of credits and non-credits, partially dynamised contributions and non-dynamised ones, and different claims to different bits of systems of post-award inflation-proofing. They cannot know, in advance, how they will stand at, say, age 45 or in different life circumstances. Nor *will* anybody or any organisation be able to inform them in total. No one will be responsible.

This issue of 'the right to know' (and with it the right to appeal) will be one challenge to the occupational pension sector. Another – and of a different order – relates to the administrative costs and the administrative chaos which will be generated with the growth of some 65,000 different occupational pension schemes and their 'in-and-out' relationships with the Reserve Scheme. This Scheme of course, if the recent political past is any guide with its denigration of government and governmental bureaucracies, will become the administrative scapegoat for the administrative delinquencies of the insurance companies and the self-assured private occupational pension schemes.

9

Public Services and Public Responsibility

In Chapter 6 we considered the role of the courts and in Chapter 7 the role of insurance as agents for redistribution and for transferring social costs. In the last chapter we examined the two British pension plans to illustrate in depth the full implications of different social values. In this chapter we return once more to the objectives of social policy and examine the role of government as an agency for carrying social costs.

At this stage, it will be helpful to look once more at our three models of social policy: Model A: *The Residual Welfare Model*; Model B: *The Industrial Achievement-Performance Model*; Model C: *The Institutional Redistributive Model*.

In the first two models (A and B), a dominant role is played by private market institutions as well as by the law – particularly in the fields of income maintenance, housing and medical care in old age, widowhood, sickness, industrial injury, unemployment, childhood and other situations of dependency. In Model A, *The Residual Welfare Model*, only a marginal role is allotted to government – to collective social policies – and then only in respect of an assumed small proportion of the population – the very poor or public assistance sector. There is, therefore, some element of redistribution or transfer payments built into this model – a relatively small flow from the generality of the population to the public assistance sector after a test of means.

For the rest of the population the model assumes that their income maintenance needs in situations of dependency will be met, on market principles, through various private institutional channels. These channels will, in effect, operate redistributive systems – on the 'worth' and 'work' maxims of distributive justice – but the assumption is made only in terms of the individual. Each individual in the system is thus assumed to take out only what he puts in – the individualistic ethic of private social policies. The Keynesian concept of 'waiting' as an economic sacrifice underlies these assumptions. Those who 'wait', who resist the animal temptations to consume in present gratifications and save (for old age, for home ownership, for unborn grandchildren and so on), must, at the very least, take out what they themselves put in. There must be, therefore, in these private social policies and institutions no element of unmerited subsidy for other individuals. Otherwise, there would be no incentive to 'wait' and defer gratification into a future Social Time.

Another assumption which has crept into this Model, alongside the one that there should be no unmerited subsidy for others, is that those who 'wait' should be given, so to speak, a special bonus from the State – from government and the generality of the population – as a reward for 'waiting' and 'saving'. In Britain as in other countries there is an extensive system of bonuses (or subsidies) of this kind – generally operated through the fiscal system as tax deductibles – for home-ownership, life assurance and other forms of saving, occupational pension schemes and so forth. At this stage, however, the particular point to note is that redistribution does actually take place in part of the private market sector as a direct result of government intervention to provide incentives to save, to acquire property and to work harder among the tax-paying population.

In both our first two models, therefore, the Residual Welfare (or Public Assistance) Model and the Achievement-Performance (Reward) Model, governments do intervene –

they do influence and change the pattern of distribution set by market forces. One particular field in which all governments in modern society intervene – or are to an increasing extent expected to intervene and to devote a large proportion of their budgets – is the provision of an immense range of what are conventionally called public amenity services. These have both positive and negative aspects. For example: town and country planning, public transport, car parks and meters, roads, recreation facilities and parks, sewage, sanitation, water, anti-air pollution subsidies, anti-noise subsidies, anti-violence measures (such as damage-proof phone boxes and more police to control football crowds, pop festivals[1]), public libraries, art galleries, museums, even Covent Garden Opera and Ballet (heavily subsidised) – an endless list indeed of social environmental, aesthetic and amenity provisions which are paid for or subsidised by the whole community. It must not, however, be assumed that the actual provision of more of these so-called public services necessarily leads to an improvement in the social and physical environment. They may simply be a brake on increasing deterioration.

How does one draw a distinction – and should one draw a distinction – between collectively organised social services and collectively organised public services? In short, what is a 'social service' and what is a 'public service'? In some respects, these two terms can be said to be almost interchangeable. Or it can be argued that all services that are collectively organised and paid for should be described as 'public services'. There is today an immense range of services that have to be provided for *everyone* if they are to be provided for *anyone*, and many of them must be paid for collectively or they cannot be had at all. How do we identify those that are social?

In the past in Britain (the story is different in other countries) the labels of 'social' and 'public' have largely been acquired in a haphazard manner. They have been applied as a result of

[1] The cost to public funds of provisions for the large 'pop' festival held in the Isle of Wight in 1969 was estimated to be £70,000.

changes in the functions of particular government departments and local agencies, as a result of different methods of book-keeping and national accounting, and as a consequence of changes in public opinion. When we put under a microscope the national accounts,[1] we find some very odd classifications. For example, in Great Britain in terms of national government expenditure, public museums and university education are social services; the London School of Economics is a social service; Eton and Harrow are publicly subsidised charities; but the probation service is not 'a social service' (presumably because it comes under the Home Office). Equally odd is the fact that the training of doctors is classified as a social service whilst the Youth Employment Service is not (presumably because it is a function of the Department of Employment). When one indulges in this sort of exercise – which can be important in measuring changes in public expenditure in the field of social policy – it would seem that no consistent principle obtains in the operational definition of a 'social service'.

In theory – in contrast to what actually happens in practice – it is possible to make certain broad distinctions in the area of services in kind. (There is less difficulty with services in cash or transfer payments as we can more generally identify the recipients.) We can distinguish between:

1. Those services that are for the individual's benefit alone, and that are provided irrespective of the individual's way of life and whether or not such services will benefit the community as a whole. The provision of home helps for old-age pensioners is an example here. They are personal, direct and are not provided in the interests of productivity. They are provided on the basis of need unrelated to merit or work performance.

2. Those services which benefit the individual and also the community, for example, medical care in cases of venereal

---

[1] Published by the Central Statistical Office in the annual 'blue book', *National Income and Expenditure*.

disease. There is an obvious community interest here (which cannot be bought in the private market) in preventing the spread of such diseases. Statistics collected by the World Health Organisation for 1969 showed that in Britain and certain other countries gonorrhoea is now completely out of control. In terms of the number of reported cases (rising by 50 per cent a year in London and other cities) gonorrhoea is now the second or third most important infectious disease in Britain and is thus pre-empting an increasing share of the resources devoted to the National Health Service. In the United States gonorrhoea is the most common infectious disease, other than the common cold. It is thus an example – the demand for abortion being another 'growth industry'[1] – of how changing social values determine priorities in social policy and contribute to our confusions over ends and means. What is also interesting is that this public health explosion has been totally unexpected. Sociologists – some of whom claim for their discipline the ability to predict within limits major changes in the behaviour of human groups – have, in all their researches, made no contribution to prediction in this field.

3. Those services that are thought to be beneficial to the community but that are not necessarily regarded as beneficial by the individual, for example, the probation service. Here we have a 'law and order' (or social control) interest combined with the provision of an individual casework service.

4. Those services that are regarded as of benefit to the community – like town planning and parks – but whose benefits cannot be attributed to any one individual. Such services are non-discriminating. We cannot discriminate, in terms of costs and benefits, between users and non-users. The same principles apply, of course, to a whole range of services like traffic control, law and order, fire brigades, public health standards in factories, offices and other buildings, the fluoridation of water

[1] See *British Medical Journal*, 31 July 1971.

supplies, and so forth. Even when charges in some cases could be levied on those who can be identified as users of the service – or on those who cause or create the disservice – we have to face the fact today that it may be uneconomic to do so; that the actual costs of collecting may exceed the benefit gained.

These four categories can be of some help in distinguishing between 'social services' and 'public services'. The most important criterion to apply is the discriminating, individualised function as opposed to the indiscriminate, impersonalised function. But in an increasingly complex and specialising society, it becomes harder to draw the line between these functions.

There are many forces at work in all modern societies – economic, technological and sociological – which tend to blur the distinction, complicate the picture, between these two concepts of personal, discriminating services and impersonal, non-discriminating services. These forces are important not just because they are relevant to the academic exercise of defining fields and making labels and classifications, but because a better understanding of the nature of these forces should help us to identify the roles and functions of social policies. It should even shed some light on the causes of inequality and deprivation and, consequently, on the problems of the distribution and redistribution of command-over-resources-in-time. It should also assist us in being more critical when we analyse different social policies.

Governments intervene not only by providing public and social services but by fiscal policy. Taxation is needed to finance public services but the distribution of tax burdens between individuals and families is itself part of social policy. This can be illustrated by examining briefly the role of direct taxes – the personal income tax, including such individual taxes as National Insurance contributions.

Less than seventy years ago direct taxation affected only a very small proportion of the total population – chiefly to pay for defence, for the British Empire, for 'law and order' and the protection of property (like fire brigades), and for a limited amount of public assistance (which, in fact, was often justified in those days as public order expenditure).

Today, in Britain, income tax has become a mass tax. It affects over 90 per cent of British families. It reaches down below the level of what we call the 'subsistence level' or the 'poverty line', namely the level of benefits and allowances set by Parliament and operated by the Supplementary Benefits Commission.[1] It is thus debatable that, partly because of the policy of the Labour Government in raising the poverty line faster than the cost of living and faster than net take-home pay of the average industrial worker, either the poverty line is too high in Britain or the tax threshold is too low. If these Supplementary Benefits were taxable (which they are not) a sizable proportion of those receiving these benefits would have their standard of living reduced by paying tax.

Poorer people are also resorting to various forms of tax evasion, such as 'moonlighting' (or two jobs), the conversion of cash income into benefits in kind, undisclosed earnings, and so on. This factor of tax evasion and avoidance among low-income earners probably provides one of the reasons for the failure of the present Government's 'take up' campaign for Family Income Supplement and other benefits. To 'take-up' these benefits means disclosing the gross earnings from all sources by both husband and wife (which also means husbands disclosing to wives what they really earn in an age of inflation and *vice versa*).

But in adopting these behaviour patterns of tax avoidance and evasion, low-income earners are only following and imitating the behaviour of those who are better off, those they admire and those they aspire to be like both in material standards and styles of life. The extent of avoidance and evasion of

[1] The extent to which those with earned incomes just above S.B.C. standards are in fact being taxed into poverty has been illustrated by Piachaud, D., 'Poverty and Taxation', *Political Quarterly*, Jan.–March 1971.

income tax and estate duty by the self-employed, the entre-
preneurs and the elderly rich has been well documented in a
number of studies in recent years. Similar patterns of tax
avoidence among the new rich – many of whom are under the
age of 30 – have not been studied so extensively. However, it
has been reported that the accumulated fortunes earned by two
'pop' groups now exceed £150 million. The fortune of one
group, The Rolling Stones, now exceeds £80 million.[1] They
have now removed themselves from Britain to the South of
France with their capital. According to the *Evening Standard*,
they have contracted out in order to avoid taxation.[2] By the
move they can avoid income tax, capital gains tax, national insurance contributions and estate duty. The loss of revenue to
the Treasury from this one pop group alone might – if it had
not been lost – have greatly eased the plight of all unmarried mothers in Britain under the age of 20.

By contrast, tax avoidance among low-paid earners and
small shop-keepers is relatively small – perhaps 50p to £1·50 a
week. No one wants to pay income tax; there are no pressure
groups calling for higher taxation on themselves; there are no
protest movements among the privileged arguing for their
privileges to be reduced. This is not what is argued by the
British Medical Association, the Association of University
Teachers or the National Union of Students. That being so, it
is not surprising that the behaviour of elites – and particularly
the admired elites in modern society – is imitated and legitimated by those who materially are much less well-off.

In terms of some of the principles of equity, these illustrations are important. The basic fact is that income tax in Britain
has now virtually acquired the characteristics of 'universality';
it has become a mass tax. The implications of this change are
far-reaching. Compared, for example, with the situation in the
1930s it is now much harder to argue that fiscal policy and
social policy are two quite separate, distinctive animals; that

[1] *Evening Standard*, 4 March 1971.
[2] *Ibid.*

there are no connections between them in the way they influence the circumstances of individuals and families. Indeed if, as now seems likely, a tax credit is introduced, income tax will become a comprehensive tax on nearly all earnings and the tax credit or allowance will become the principal vehicle for social policy transfers among those at work.[1]

It was argued – and, indeed, is still argued by some authorities like Professor Friedman of Chicago and other advocates of negative income tax – that fiscal policy is (or should be) neutral, politically and socially neutral, in the sacrifices it entails. In short, government should extract minimum taxes (progressive or proportionate) from the whole population; it should abolish 'selectivity' in the system by giving negative tax allowances, like child allowances, to poor people and, thereafter, everyone should be free to spend their money as they like and to have freedom of choice to buy education, medical care, housing and social services in the private market place.

Ultimately, of course, this view implies the 'withering away' of State intervention and of bureaucratic 'Welfare States' and social policy institutions. Coming from Professor Friedman and various neo-classical economists, it is curiously Marxist in its dialectic and paradoxically anarchist in its philosophy – and reminiscent of the writings of Professor Marcuse and of Professor Charles Reich's book *The Greening of America*.[2] The argument of this book is well known; but I will summarise it for those who have not read it.

The Corporate State in the USA has hitherto been sustained by two types of consciousness, the selfish consciousness of small-town America that encourages each man to improve himself and his family at the expense of others (personalised diswelfares), and the liberal consciousness of the technocrat

---

[1] *Proposals for a Tax Credit System*, Cmnd. 5116, HMSO, 1972.
[2] Reich, C., *The Greening of America*, Allen Lane, London, 1971; Penguin, Harmondsworth, 1972.

(or social engineer) who reads the *New York Times*, has his clothes made in England and supposes that social problems can be cured by economic growth plus national planning imposed by a managerial elite or establishment. But the Corporate State will destroy itself, argues Professor Reich, by producing a new consciousness – consciousness III – which already shows itself in those Yale undergraduates among whom Professor Reich lives and works, and which soon must become an epidemic. This consciousness expresses itself in experimentation with clothing, sex, music and drugs; its fundamental principles are spontaneity, freedom, love and the peace and tolerance that these other virtues must inevitably bring. It is therefore unnecessary to work to improve America, it is only necessary for each man (or woman) to do his thing, as Consciousness III spreads contagiously from Yale to the suburbs and from the suburbs to the factories and the ghettos.

This thesis has made everyone happy, this charming confection of Galbraith, Friedman and the Brothers Grimm. Especially middle-class parents are glad to be proud of their bizarre children once again, and happy to strike a blow for social justice by switching from gin to pot. It made everyone happy – particularly citizens like Governor Wallace of Alabama and Governor Reagan of California on the political right protesting for less government, less welfare and fewer bureaucrats – except for those people who believed that if everyone cultivates his own garden (black as well as white) no one will cultivate anything else. The market will reign supreme as beneficent growth allows everyone to do their thing.

It will follow, therefore, that such institutions as medical care, education and other social services in kind will come to be treated as consumption goods – they will be 'reprivatised' or liberated from State bureaucracy. This is not the place to get involved in all the complex issues of debating whether and to what extent medical care and other services are or are not consumption goods like cars or refrigerators. Professor Lees and other writers have argued that they should be so treated in

Freedom or Free-for-all[1] and other publications by the Institute of Economic Affairs. A fundamentally different point of view is to be found in *The Gift Relationship*.[2]

Once again we see that social policy is all about social purposes and choices between them. These choices – and the conflicts between them involving simultaneously the means–ends equation – have continuously to be made at the collective (governmental level), the community level and the individual level. At each level, by acting or not acting, by voting or not voting, by opting in or contracting out, we can influence the direction in which choices are made. Individual or group neutrality is not attainable. There can be no such thing as a 'neutral' taxation system.

Society has to make choices – that is to say, we all have to make choices – between more government or more markets; more freedom for some at the expense of other people's freedom; more social justice for some and less freedom for others; and so on.

At the heart of many of these choices concerning the central question of the politics of the good society – the question of obedience or coercion – lies the conflict between individual equity and social equality. In each, and between each, of our three models the conflict is there – a conflict often presenting itself in the dilemmas of altruism and egoism.

[1] Lees, D., *Freedom or Free-for-all*, Hobart Papers, Vol. 3, Institute of Economic Affairs, London, 1965.

[2] Titmuss, R. M., *The Gift Relationship*, Allen & Unwin, London, 1970.

10

Values and Choices

There is no escape from value choices in welfare systems. The construction of any models or the elaboration of any theories which have anything to do with 'policy' must inevitably be concerned with 'what is and what might be'; with what we (as members of a society) want (the ends); and with how we get there (the means).

Not only is 'policy' all about values but those who discuss problems of policy have their own values (some would call them prejudices). But, whatever they are called, it is obvious that the social sciences – and particularly economics and sociology – are not, nor can ever be, 'value free'. No doubt there are some practitioners, concerned about the professional status of their subject or discipline (which in itself is an odd word suggestive of a master-servant relationship), who like to think they are value-free, floating in an abstracted social world of an exact Robinson Crusoe science. They take refuge in the description of facts, or in mathematical model-building, or in a mystique of casework or psycho-analysis. But even the labelling of one's subject or the choice of topics for research or for teaching in the social sciences can reveal the existence of value premises. Consider the use of such terms as 'race relations'. Does it not imply certain judgements about the unscientific concept of race? Or the use of such valuative and emotive terms as 'economic growth', 'progress', 'productivity', 'health', 'social mobility', 'equality' and so forth?

There are, of course, some social phenomena that may be studied with a certain degree of cold rational disinterestedness while never achieving the lack of involvement displayed by a mathematician analysing a quadratic equation. But this is not possible with the study of social policy or, to take another example, social deviation – a concept which is inextricably mixed up in all fields of social policy, medical care, social work and psychiatry. One of the value assumptions, for instance, concealed in Model A – *The Residual Welfare Model of Social Policy* – is that the residual non-market sector (the public social policy sector) should concern itself with the social deviants; the 'bad actuarial risks', those who are unwilling or unable to provide for their own needs – and the needs of their families – through the normal mechanisms of the market.

The definition of deviation means an aberration, turning from the right course, obliquity of conduct. Language is not a mere symbolic tool of communication. By describing someone as deviant we express an attitude; we morally brand him and stigmatise him with our value judgement. Social deviation, like crime, is a social ill or a 'social problem'. The ultimate aim of some people who study the aetiology and pressures leading to crime and deviation is to devise better ways and means to combat and prevent them. This stems from a clear-cut value involvement.

The investigators of *The Power Elite*,[1] *The Status Seekers*[2] and *The Hidden Persuaders*[3] were hardly neutral towards their subjects. Less obvious is the higher proportion of Jews to non-Jews among the investigators of anti-Semitism. Merton[4] may have partially escaped the perils of value judgement be-

---

[1] Mills, C. W., *The Power Elite*, Oxford University Press, New York, 1956.

[2] Packard, V. O., *The Status Seekers*, Longman, London; Penguin, Harmondsworth, 1971.

[3] Packard, V. O., *The Hidden Persuaders*, Longman, London; Penguin, Harmondsworth, 1970.

[4] Merton, R. K., *Social Theory and Social Structure*, Glencoe, Free Press, 1957.

cause he was mainly concerned with the schematic description and typology of deviants; but many others have not. They have followed the original Durkheimian conception of deviance according to which the unadjusted, the pariahs, the outsiders, are by definition detrimental to the interests of the group, and their faulty solidarity invariably injures the group itself.

Consequently, one of the vital norms of every group is that the individuals comprising it should 'adjust' or conform to its normative system and values. The term 'adjustment' in itself is associated immediately with the use of power and pressure to chip off the corners of a square peg so that it fits into a round hole.

Actually, 'adjustment' is a virtue prescribed by the group whose interest (i.e. solidarity) it serves, which has the power to enforce it and apply sanctions to those who are maladjusted. The analysis of the processes leading to deviation in the Durkheimian tradition is necessarily based on an axiomatic value judgement – that group cohesion solidarity and following group norms is 'functional', social (as opposed to anti-social) and therefore *good*!

The whole 'adjustment' literature in the socio-psychological, psychiatric and educational fields is based on this axiomatic premise. The image of a balanced personality, one who 'plays according to the rules of the game' prescribed by the group norms, is a direct corollary of this premise.

'The rules of the game', explicit or implicit in our three different models of social policy, are values which we all have to think about, criticise and argue about. There is no imperative 'ought' or 'should' or 'rightness' about any one of them. The social sciences cannot give a final answer to the question whether any given policy is 'right'. On the other hand, the social scientist can study what people say they want, what they think they want, and may even infer from their behaviour what they 'really' want, but it is not the business of science to say whether people want the *right* things. The critique of ends –

that is, the discussion of what are the right things to want – is more in the province of the philosopher or the theologian. But who today qualifies as a philosopher – people like Sartre who summed up in his play *No Exit*: 'Hell is other people'?[1]

This, however, is not to say that those who study social policy cannot make any contribution at all to the discussion of objectives. They can point out, for instance, that many things that people think are ends are, in fact, means to some further end, and that a discussion that seems to be about ends (like our models of social policy) may be more easily resolved if it can be stated in terms of a choice of means to some further end. They may also point out that human activity seldom has but one objective, and that there are many ends, some of which may not be compatible.

The Americans want safe and effective surgical operations, but they do not want to support free and anonymous blood donations to minimise the risks of serum hepatitis. We (as well as the Americans) want to diminish colour prejudice but we do not always want social policies that are non-discriminatory in character. We want riches but we also want the things that make for poverty – the social costs, damages and disservices of economic growth. We want equality but we also want wage and salary differentials. We want to be paid more when we are working than when we are not working, yet at the same time we want to abolish the wage-stop. And who are the 'we' in all this – what are the boundaries of my and other people's welfare: the family, the kin, the village, the state or the world? Where does egoism end and altruism begin? Should we import human blood from other societies, or even recruit doctors from poorer nations because we (or the United States or Canada) have discovered that, in the international medical market place, it is now cheaper to import doctors than to train them?

So far as the study of these social policy questions is

---

[1] Sartre, J. P., 'In Camera' ('Huis Clos') trans. Gilbert, S. in Browne, E. M. (ed), *Three European Plays*, Penguin, Harmondsworth, 1948, p. 191.

concerned, all we can do is to expose more clearly the value choices confronting society – whether they relate to medical care, social security, education and other services which, in essence, involve social relations and systems of belief. As Joan Robinson once said in discussing the value premises of economics, 'without ideology we would never have thought of the question(s)'.[1] And so it is with social policy models which, with all their apparent remoteness from reality, can serve a purpose in providing us with an ideological framework which may stimulate us to ask the significant questions and expose the significant choices.

We will not be led to ask the significant questions if we view the area of social policy as (so to speak) a closed and separate system of welfare for a particular group or groups in society. Or as a technical exercise in social engineering in which a power elite decides, in a closed system, how much welfare poor people need, and how it should be provided. As soon as we narrow our vision in this way we are at once in danger of being imprisoned in one of the stereotypes associated with the notion of 'The Welfare State' or a 'War on Poverty'. Assumptions here include those that 'welfare' is necessarily and inevitably improving (as the Victorians would have said), or wholly beneficent (as some left-wing politicians believe) or an adjustable fringe donation (as some right-wing politicians believe). Or again, that what *we* do for *poor* people or *to* poor people (which in itself raises the question of how we identify the poor and how we discriminate in their favour) will inevitably lead us – if we win the poverty war – to some sort of final welfare destination. It sounds simple – too simple; the conversion of the poor into the non-poor.

This is, perhaps, an unjust criticism, because all generalisations – like generalisations about 'The Welfare State' or 'Wars on Poverty' – have a common drawback: both ends and means are made to appear deceptively simple. It is when we move from abstract generalisation to the precise diagnosis of social

[1] Robinson, J., *Economic Philosophy*, Watts, London, 1962, p. 4.

problems that the trouble begins. It is at this point we have to ask the significant questions, and we are unlikely to do so unless our conceptual frame of reference (as well as our world of reality) includes the non-poor as well as the poor; the uncertainties of social change as well as the certainties; the past and the future in the spectrum of social time as well as the present.

The social services (in cash and in kind) need to be seen, not as a single system of welfare with a single objective, but as a number of systems with a variety of objectives, some in harmony, some in conflict with each other. There are in Britain, as in many other countries, essentially three different systems of 'social services': Social Welfare, Fiscal Welfare and Occupational Welfare.[1]

The first system, Social Welfare, includes all those directly administered services and transfer payments classified by the Treasury for expenditure purposes under the rubric 'The Social Services'. These cover what are conventionally known as 'social services', organised and administered by central, regional and local authorities (and including grants to voluntary agencies for delegated services like Citizens' Advice Bureaux) – for example, primary and secondary education, the National Health Service, social security payments, local authority housing and many others.

In the public view, these are 'the social services' – the observable part of welfare phenomena. Considered historically, however, the term 'the social services' has come to be applied to more and more areas of collective provision for certain 'needs'. It has indeed acquired a most elastic quality; its expanding frontiers, formerly enclosing little besides poor relief, sanitation and public nuisances at the beginning of the century, now embrace a multitude of heterogeneous activities, some recognised by the public as social services and some not.

The system of Fiscal Welfare relates, in total, to reliefs,

---

[1] This theme is developed in greater length in Titmuss, R. M., 'The Social Division of Welfare', *Essays on the 'Welfare State'*, 2nd ed., Allen & Unwin, London, 1963.

allowances and deductions under direct systems of taxation, central and local, and such 'taxes' as National Insurance (or social security) so-called contributions.

Under separately administered social security systems, like family allowances and retirement pensions, direct cash payments are made in discharging collective responsibilities for particular dependencies. In the relevant accounts, these are treated as 'social service' expenditure since they represent flows of payments through the central government account. Allowances and reliefs from income tax, though providing similar benefits and expressing a similar social purpose in the recognition of dependent needs, are not, however, treated as social service expenditure. The first is a cash transaction; the second an accounting convenience. Despite this difference in administrative method, the tax saving that accrues to the individual is, in effect, a transfer payment. As an American economist pointed out: 'By reducing the tax liability of a person with dependants the State is sharing the responsibility of caring for each taxpayer's family just as certainly as if it were paying cash allowances in each case.'[1]

In their primary objectives and their effects on individual purchasing power there are basic similarities in these two ways by which collective provision is made for dependencies. Both are manifestations of social policies in favour of identified groups in the population and both reflect changes in public opinion in regard to the relationship between the State, the individual and the family.

Since the introduction of progressive taxation in 1907 there has been a remarkable development of social policy operating through the medium of the fiscal system. This has chiefly taken the form of increasing support for the family through the recognition of more types of dependencies and substantial additions to the value of the benefits provided. Another important aspect of this development is that, originally, these

---

[1] Cartter, A. M., 'Income Tax Allowances and the Family in Great Britain', *Population Studies*, Vol. VI, No. 3, 1953, p. 219.

dependants' benefits were deliberately restricted to the lowest paid sections of the income tax population; in the course of time these restrictions have disappeared.

Fiscal welfare includes in its scope a large area of 'needs' and 'dependencies' in addition to family endowment and 'self-improvement'. It would be tedious to discuss them here – the list is a long one and includes: saving for old age; life assurance and superannuation allowances; allowances for aged, incapacitated and infirm kinship dependants; housekeepers for professional women; mortgage allowances for owner-occupiers; interest on bank loans for those living on credit (a different concept of 'waiting'); contributions to charities; subsidies for public school education; private medical care; family trusts, covenants and so forth.

During much the same period of time that has witnessed many developments in social and fiscal welfare policies there has also occurred a great expansion in occupational welfare benefits in cash and in kind. They have now reached formidable and widespread proportions as the Royal Commission on Taxation recognised in 1955.[1] Although they are provided by employers (mainly, it should be noted, for regularly employed men) the cost (probably to the extent of about one-half) falls on the whole body of taxpayers because they are tax deductibles. They include not only occupational pensions but child allowances; death benefits, health and welfare services; personal expenses for travel, entertainment, dress and equipment; meal vouchers; motor cars and season tickets; residential accommodation; holiday expenses; children's school fees; sickness benefits; medical expenses; education and training grants; cheap meals; unemployment benefit; medical bills and an incalculable variety of benefits in kind ranging from 'obvious forms of realizable goods to the most intangible forms of amenity'.[2]

---

[1] *Royal Commission on Taxation of Income and Profits* (Final Report), Cmnd. 9474, HMSO, p. 55.
[2] *Ibid.*, p. 68.

The implications of this trend in Occupational Welfare were cautiously remarked on by the Royal Commission:

'Modern improvements in the conditions of employment and the recognition by employers of a wide range of obligations towards the health, comfort and amenities of their staff may well lead to a greater proportion of an employee's true remuneration being expressed in a form that is neither money nor convertible into money.'[1]

A substantial part of all these multifarious benefits can be interpreted as the recognition of dependencies; the dependencies of old age, of sickness and incapacity, of childhood, widowhood and so forth. They are in effect, if not in administrative method, 'social services', duplicating and overlapping social and fiscal welfare benefits. The rapidity of their growth in recent years has increasingly diminished the value and relevance of salary, wage and income statistics.

No doubt many of these forms of occupational social services express the desire for 'good human relations' in industry. Their provision is part of the image of the 'good' employer. They are also deeply embedded in the principle of meeting social needs on the basis of work performance, occupational achievement and productivity. In this sense they form a major part of our second Model of Social Policy – Model B: *The Industrial Achievement-Performance Model of Social Policy.*

Some of the questions which have to be examined in relation to this Model of Social Policy include:

1. What effect does this system of occupational welfare have on the distribution of command-over-resources-in-time for the whole population – for the non-employed as well as the employed?

2. What effect does the system have on the social and psycho-

1 *Ibid.*, p. 72.

logical sense of community? Does it have divisive or unifying effects and in what sense and for what groups? Does it, in short, widen or diminish the concept and consciousness of 'who is my neighbour'?

3. To what extent (and in comparison with other systems of welfare) does occupational welfare provide both freedom of choice in welfare benefits (pensions, medical care and so forth) and a sense of participation in the organisation and administration of the system.

We cannot generalise in any rational way about the respective roles and functions of government and the private sector unless we have first considered questions of this kind.

Among all the theories and principles relating to social policy, particularly with respect to our three disparate and elusive models, perhaps the most fundamental ones centre round the historic problems of distributive justice. They embrace four well-known maxims:

> 1. To each according to his *need.*
> 2. To each according to his *worth.*
> 3. To each according to his *merit.*
> 4. To each according to his *work.*

To these four we might add a fifth: To each according to *our needs.* In other words, if it is the will of society to move towards a more equal society, which of these four maxims should determine the provision of welfare?

POSTSCRIPT

POSTSCRIPT

I was sitting on a bench with five other people in the outpatient visiting space of the Radiotherapy Department of the Westminster Hospital in London. We were all booked in by appointment at 10 o'clock daily week after week to go into a room called the Theratron Room. I'll explain what that means a bit later on. Next to me on the bench there was a harassed middle-aged woman, married to a postman, who had two children and who lived somewhere near a ghastly part of London called Tooting Broadway. She, like the others, had been brought to the Westminster Hospital by ambulance. She was suffering from cancer of the pelvis.

We talked, as we talked every morning, amongst ourselves and about ourselves and she suddenly said to me, 'You know, the doctors say I should rest as much as I can but I really can't do so.' I said to her, 'Why not?' And she said, 'Well, you see I haven't dared tell the neighbours that I've got cancer. They think it's infectious. Anyway, it's not very respectable, is it, to have cancer?' And then she said, 'You wouldn't tell your students would you?' By then, of course, she knew me and she knew I came from a strange, peculiar place called the London School of Economics where she thought a lot of strange, peculiar students had a lovely time at the taxpayers' expense. My answer to her was, 'Of course. Of course I would tell them; why shouldn't I use six-letter words? They can use four-letter words. Don't you know cancer is not infectious? And it is respectable. Even professors get cancer.' So you see I had to keep a promise I gave her before Christmas.

For many months last year I had experienced an acute, frustrating and annoying pain in my right shoulder and my right arm. This prevented me from doing a lot of things I wanted to do. And, incidentally, it made it difficult for me to concentrate. It began long before the examination period and you know there is one rule that I think students might think about which is that no professor or any teacher at the university who is suffering from any kind of pain (perhaps stress is a better word) should be allowed to mark examination scripts. Anyway, apart from all that, through my local National Health Service general practitioner and my local hospital I went through a series of X-rays, tests of various kinds and they all came out with the answer that my trouble was muscular skeletal – something which the doctors in their shorthand called a 'frozen shoulder'. Later I learned that there is considerable doubt about the causes or cures or reasons for 'frozen shoulders', just as there is about a condition known as 'low back pain' among the working classes. However, with this diagnosis I was fed into the physiotherapy department of our local hospital where I did exercises. I underwent very painful treatment of various kinds and in spite of all this and doing what I was told the pain got worse and it wouldn't go away.

Eventually, and to cut a long story short, I found myself being admitted as a National Health Service patient at 3 o'clock on Saturday, the 30th of September 1972, as an inpatient at the Westminster Hospital. Admission on a Saturday afternoon seemed to me to be very odd but I did as I was told and I was informed that if I came in on a Saturday afternoon a lot of tests and X-Rays could be done on me and all would be ready for the arrival of the great men – the consultants – on Monday morning. On the Sunday, the following day, I didn't have any visitors. My wife had had to put up with a lot from me for weeks and months beforehand and so I wouldn't let her come and see me on the Sunday. By about 8 o'clock on the Sunday evening I decided that I would like to talk to her on the telephone. By then I had learned from the nursing staff that there was such a thing as a mobile telephone which could be dragged round the ward, plugged in and then you could have a private conversation. So I got hold of the mobile telephone and tried to get through. But every time I tried I found myself on a crossed line with another man talking to somebody else on the same line. After about ten to fifteen minutes a door opened from a side room near me where I was in the ward, a side room which was used on occasion for amenity patients or private patients. The door opened and out of it came a human being about three feet five inches high in the shape of a question mark. He couldn't raise his head but in a quiet voice he said to me, 'Can I help you? You're having trouble with the telephone.' So I said, 'Yes, I can't get through; I want to talk to my wife.' And he said, 'But don't you know, there are three telephones on the third floor of this ward with the same number so you are probably talking to a patient at the other end of the corridor who is probably also talking to his wife.' Well, that cleared that one up.

The man who came to help me – let's call him Bill – I got to know very well. He was aged 53. In 1939, at the age of 19, he was an apprentice engineer in Portsmouth and he was called up for the Army at the outbreak of war. In 1942 Bill got married. In 1943 he and his wife had a son, their only child. In 1944 Bill was blown up in the desert by Rommel and his back was broken in about six places. Somehow or other in 1944 in a military hospital they put him together again and he eventually came under the responsibility of a war pensioners' hospital attached to the Westminster. Since the National Health Service came into operation in 1948 Bill has spent varying periods from two to four or five weeks every year at the Westminster Hospital receiving the latest micro developments for the care and rehabilitation of people like Bill. He has never worked.

Bill and I one night worked out roughly what he had cost the National Health Service since 1948. When he was due for treatment, they sent for him by ambulance from Portsmouth where he lived in a council house and they took him back. The amount was something like a quarter of a million pounds. Now Bill was a passionate gardener – that was one of his great interests in life. While I was at the Westminster a book was published by a friend of mine, Pat Hamilton [Lady Hamilton of the Disabled Living Foundation]. This book called *Gardening for the Disabled* is a great help to seriously disabled people in carrying on a hobby like gardening. Within two days of the book's publication the mobile voluntarily-staffed library at the Westminster Hospital, remembering Bill's interest in gardening, sent up to him the book to read. Bill in his side room was equipped with a small television set. I joined him because while I was in the Westminster the Labour Party Conference was being held in Blackpool and I attended it, at least in spirit, most of the time. It wasn't easy to concentrate. A hospital ward between the hours of about 8 o'clock in the morning and 6 o'clock in the evening is as busy with traffic as Piccadilly Circus. There is always somebody coming in to do something. There's the mobile shop that turns up twice a day; there is the mobile library that turns up once a day;

there are the people who come in to take your temperature, the student nurse who brings you the menu card for the next twenty-four hours and comes to collect it after you've decided between roast beef and chicken *vol-au-vent* for supper tomorrow; the people who come in to give you clean water; there is the lady from Brixton, homesick for Trinidad, who brings in a very noisy vacuum cleaner. And when I said to her, 'Please, take it away, Bill and I are really very clean, we haven't got any dust under the bed and the Common Market debate is going on. It's the Labour Party Conference in Blackpool.' She said, 'What's the Common Market anyway – never heard of it – I've got my job to do.' Eventually I persuaded her to leave us alone in peace to follow the infighting going on in Blackpool.

After the hospital had taken about eighteen pictures from various angles of my shoulder and I had gone through a lot of other tests, I was told that what was causing all the trouble was what looked like dry rot in the top of my ribs. So they had to operate. They operated and then they had to have a conference to obtain the right histological classification of cancer. Before the operation and after the operation I had a seminar (with official permission of course) with the nursing students and I had a seminar with the medical students of one of the consultants. Somehow or other it had become known in the ward that I had written a book about blood and that I came from this strange place at LSE where many of my students became social workers. Inevitably, I was asked: What do social workers actually do? What *is* a social administrator? Two days after my operation I was allowed by the medical staff, by the house officers and the registrars, by the hierarchy in general to go down to the 'Paviour's Arms' with some of the old-age pensioners where they had a pint of beer at 7 o'clock in the evening and I had a whisky. And I was also allowed to go out to a little restaurant in Ebury Street for dinner with friends and members of the staff of the Social Administration Department. So you see hospitals are flexible and this is an area where the middle classes can often get the best out of the social services. I am, I suppose, middle class. I am, I suppose, articulate whereas many of the patients are not.

After my discharge as an inpatient from the Westminster Hospital it was rather a moving experience because some of the staff of the Supplementary Benefits Commission had sent me a sort of miniature Rochford rockery and, in a little ceremony in the ward, I handed over the rockery to Bill and the staff were arranging for it to go home with him to Portsmouth and I also handed over copies of my book, *The Gift Relationship*, to the Nurses' Library and the Medical Students' Library. I think one of the best compliments I was paid as an inpatient was when I was helping two of the student nurses to make my bed one morning. They knew where I came from – they thought I was an authority on matters of this kind – and they said to me, 'We've been having an argument in the hostel about the right age to get married. What do you think, Professor? When do you think young people should get married?' Well, I really had no answer – all I could say was 'Not too soon and please not too late.'

After my discharge, I and other cancer patients had to attend every day for five to six weeks for radium treatment from a Cobalt 60 theratron machine. Capital expenditure cost was about half a million pounds and there are not many of these machines in London and the South-East. I began with an exposure of eight minutes which gradually mounted to about twenty-five minutes. I can only describe this machine by saying that as you went into the theratron room you walked past a control panel which looked like what I imagine might resemble the control panel of the Concorde cockpit. After that, you lie almost naked on a machine and you are raised and lowered and this machine beams at you from various angles radium at a cost, so I am told, of about £10 per minute. I had in all about seventeen hours. In addition, while one was on the machine, the National Health Service kindly supplied piped music free of charge in order to help patients relax.

Now, as you will have gathered from what I have said, I was extraordinarily lucky. It was a marvellous ward, staffed by some very interesting people looking after an extraordinarily interesting and diverse cross-section of the British public drawn from south-east London – south-east England in fact. If all wards in all the hospitals all over the country were anywhere near the standard of this ward at the Westminster we should have very little to complain about in evaluating standards of performance of the National Health Service. But you know, as well as I know, that not all wards are like the ward that I was in.

When I went in on that Saturday afternoon I took with me John Rawls' book, *A Theory of Justice*, which I think is one of the most important books published in the field of social philosophy for the last twenty-five years. I took that with me and I took with me an advance copy of the present Government's Green Paper on Tax Credits, and I also took a bottle of whisky. Anyway, I can tell you that while I was there I didn't get very far with *A Theory of Justice*; there wasn't time, there was too much to do, there were too many people to talk to; one had to help – one liked to help – with the tea trolley at 6 o'clock in the morning, when all the mobile patients served the immobile patients, and one shuffled around not caring what one looked like and learning a great deal about other human beings and their predicaments. But I did read the Green Paper on Tax Credits and, I don't suppose it happens very often, I did write a letter to the Editor of *The Times* from the Westminster Hospital – he didn't know it came from the hospital because I signed it from my home – about the Green Paper because I thought then, indeed I still think, that the proposals, rough as they are, have considerable potentialities for extending some of the benefits of the welfare state from the middle classes downwards to the poor.

In some of the things that I have said and in some of the things that I have written in some of my books, I have talked about what I have called 'social growth'. I believe that my experience at the Westminster provides some of the unquantifiable indicators of social growth. These are indicators that cannot be measured, cannot be quantified, but relate to the texture of relationships between human beings. These indicators cannot be calculated. They are not, as my friends the economists tell me, counted in all the Blue Books and in all the publications of the Central Statistical Office. For example, nowhere will you find any explanation or any statement about the expenditures by the National Health Service on my friend Bill and all the other expenditures – public housing, a constant attendance allowance, a daily home help and meals-on-wheels (his wife, aged 52, went blind last year), an invalid chair, special ramps, an adapted lavatory and kitchen, lowered sinks and raised garden beds (provided by the local Parks Department). He was an example, in practice, of what a compassionate society can achieve when a philosophy of social justice and public accountability is translated into a hundred and one detailed acts of imagination and tolerance.

Among all the other experiences I had, another which stands out is that of a young West Indian from Trinidad, aged 25, with cancer of the rectum. His appointment was the same as mine for radium treatment – 10 o'clock every day. Sometimes he went into the Theratron Room first; sometimes I did. What determined waiting was quite simply the vagaries of London traffic – not race, religion, colour or class.

BIBLIOGRAPHY

Abel-Smith, B., *The Hospitals, 1800–1948*, Heinemann, London, 1964.

Acton, H. B., *The Morals of Markets: an ethical exploration*, Longman, London, 1971.

Arrow, K. J., 'Uncertainty and the Welfare Economics of Medical Care', *American Economic Review*, Vol. LIII, No. 5, December 1963.

Atiyah, P. S., *Accidents, Compensation and the Law*, Weidenfeld & Nicolson, London, 1970.

Automobile Insurance . . . For Whose Benefit? Report to Governor Rockefeller, New York State, 1970.

Beales, H. L., *The Making of Social Policy*, Hobhouse Memorial Trust Lecture No. 15, Oxford University Press, 1945.

Berlin, I., *Four Essays on Liberty*, Oxford University Press, London, 1969.

Benn, S. I. and Peters, R. S., *Social Principles and the Democratic State*, Allen & Unwin, London, 1961.

Boulding, K. E., *Principles of Economic Policy*, Staples Press, London, 1959.

Boulding, K. E., 'The Boundaries of Social Policy', *Social Work*, Vol. 12, No. 1, 1967.

Bruce, M., *The Coming of the Welfare State*, Batsford, London, 1961.

Burns, E., *Social Security and Public Policy*, McGraw-Hill, New York, 1956.

Caplovitz, D., *The Poor Pay More*, Free Press of Glencoe, New York, 1963.

Cartter, A. M., 'Income Tax Allowances and the Family in Great Britain', *Population Studies*, Vol. VI, No. 3, 1953.

Civil Liability for Dangerous Things and Activities, Law Commission Report No. 32, House of Commons Paper 142, HMSO, 1970.

The Civil Service, Report of the Fulton Committe, 1968, Cmnd. 3638.

Cloward, R. and Fox-Piven, F., *Regulating the Poor: the functions of public welfare*, Tavistock Publications, London, 1972.

Cohn, J., *The Conscience of the Corporation*, Johns Hopkins Press, Baltimore, 1971.

Corbett, P., *Ideologies*, Hutchinson, London, 1965.

Davies, J. M., 'Bladder Tumours in the Electric Cable Industry', *Lancet*, 24 June 1965.

Dawson, R. F. F., *Current Costs of Road Accidents in Great Britain*, Road Research Laboratory, LR 396, 1971.

De Schweinitz, K., *England's Road to Social Security*, Barnes, New York, 1961.

Donnison, D. V. *et al.*, *Social Policy and Administration*, Allen & Unwin, London, 1965.

Drucker, P., *The Age of Discontinuity*, Heinemann, London, 1969.

Galbraith, J. K., *The Affluent Society*, Hamish Hamilton, London, 1958; Penguin, Harmondsworth, 1970.

Gilbert, B., *The Evolution of National Insurance in Great Britain*, Michael Joseph, London, 1966.

Gilbert, B., *British Social Policy, 1914–39*, Batsford, London, 1970.

Ginsberg, M., *The Idea of Progress: a revaluation*, Methuen, London, 1953.

Goffman, E., *Stigma: notes on the management of spoiled identity*, Penguin, Harmondsworth, 1970.

Gordon, M. S., *The Economics of Welfare Policies*, Columbia University Press, New York, 1963.

Gurvitch, G. D., *The Spectrum of Social Time*, Reidel, Holland, 1963.

Hagenbuch, W., *Social Economics*, Nisbet, Welwyn, 1958.

Hall, M. P., *The Social Services of Modern England*, Routledge & Kegan Paul, London, 1969.

Halsey, A. H. (ed), *Trends in British Society Since 1900*, Macmillan, London, 1972.

Handicapped and Impaired in Great Britain, Department of Health and Social Security, HMSO, 1971.

Harbrecht, P. P., *Pension Funds and Economic Power*, The Twentieth Century Fund, New York, 1959.

Harris, J., *Unemployment and Politics: a study in English social policy, 1886–1914*, Clarendon Press, Oxford, 1973.

Hirschman, A. O., *The Strategy of Economic Development*, Yale University Press, New Haven, 1958.

Hohaus, R. A., *The Record*, American Institute of Actuaries, June 1938.

Ison, T., *The Forensic Lottery*, Staples, London, 1967.

James, R. D., 'Three R's Inc.', *Wall Street Journal*, 2 June 1971.

Jefferys, M., *The Anatomy of Social Welfare*, Michael Joseph, London, 1965.

Jones, K., *Mental Health and Social Policy, 1845–1959*, Routledge & Kegan Paul, London, 1960.

Lafitte, F., *Social Policy in a Free Society*, Birmingham University Press, Birmingham, 1962.

Leach, E., 'Models', *New Society*, 14 May 1964.

Lees, D., *Freedom or Free-for-all?*, Hobart Papers, Vol. 3, Institute of Economic Affairs, London, 1965.

Lindsey, A., *Socialized Medicine in England and Wales*, University of North Carolina Press, Chapel Hill, 1962.

'Life with Nye', *The Observer* Colour Supplement, 10 December 1972.

Macbeath, A., *Can Social Policies be Rationally Tested?*, Hobhouse Memorial Trust lecture, Oxford University Press, 1957.

McKinsey and Co., *Report to British Insurance Association* summarised in *The Times*, 10 May 1965.

MacLeod, I. and Powell, E., *The Social Services*, Conservative Political Centre, London, 1954.

Madison, B. Q., *Social Welfare in the Soviet Union*, Stanford University Press, Stanford, 1968.

Marsh, D. C., *An Introduction to the Study of Social Administration*, Routledge & Kegan Paul, London, 1965.

Marshall, T. H., *Social Policy*, Hutchinson, University Library, London, 1965.

Marris, R. and Wood, A., *The Corporate Economy*, Macmillan, London, 1971.

Mays, J., *Growing up in the City*, University Press of Liverpool, Liverpool, 1954.

Meeting the Insurance Crisis of our Cities, a report by the President's Advisory Panel, us Government Printing Office, Washington, 1968.

Merriman, I. C., 'Overlap of Benefits under OASDI and other Programs', *Social Security Bulletin*, us Department of Health, Education and Welfare, Vol. 28, No. 4, April 1965.

Merton, R. K. and Nisbet, R. A., *Contemporary Social Problems*, Harcourt Brace & World, New York, 1961.

Merton, R. K., *Social Theory and Social Structure*, Free Press, Glencoe, 1961.

Mészáros, I., *Marx's Theory of Alienation*, Merlin Press, London, 1970.

Miller, S. M. and Roby, P. N., *The Future of Inequality*, Basic Books, New York, 1970.

Mills, C. Wright, *The Power Elite*, Oxford University Press, New York, 1956.

Mills, C. Wright, *The Sociological Imagination*, Oxford University Press, New York, 1959; Penguin, Harmondsworth, 1970.

Mishan, E. J., *The Costs of Economic Growth*, Staples Press, London, 1967.

Moore, W. E., *Social Change*, Prentice Hall, London, 1963.

Myrdal, G. et al., *An American Dilemma: the Negro problem and modern democracy*, Harper & Row, London, 1962.

Myrdal, G., *The Challenge of World Poverty*, Allen Lane, London, 1970.

Nath, S. K., *A Reappraisal of Welfare Economics*, Routledge & Kegan Paul, London, 1969.

A National Health Service, Ministry of Health, Cmnd. 6502, HMSO, 1944.

National Superannuation and Social Insurance, White Paper, HMSO, 1969

Nyerere, J. K., *Ujama: essays on socialism*, Oxford University Press, Dar es Salaam, 1968.

Occupational Pension Schemes: a new survey by the Government Actuary, Treasury, HMSO, 1966.

Packard, V. O., *The Status Seekers*, Longman, London; Penguin, Harmondsworth, 1971.

Packard, V. O., *The Hidden Persuaders*, Longman, London; Penguin, Harmondsworth, 1970.

Parsons, T. in *The Sociology of Work* (T. Caplow (ed), 1954), University of Minnesota Press, Minneapolis, 1954.

Parsons, T., *The Structure of Social Action*, Allen & Unwin, London, 1949.

Parsons, T., *The Social System*, Routledge & Kegan Paul, London, 1964.

Peacock, A., *The Welfare Society*, Liberal Publication Department, London, 1960.

Piachaud, D., 'Poverty and Taxation', *Political Quarterly*, Jan.–March 1971.

Pigou, A. C., *The Economics of Welfare*, Macmillan, London, 1920.

Pilch, M. and Wood, V., *Pension Scheme Practice*, Hutchinson, London, 1967.

Pinker, R. A., *Social Theory and Social Policy*, Heinemann, London, 1971.

Proposals for a Tax Credit System, Cmnd. 5116, HMSO, 1972.

Public Health Guidelines for large Pop Festivals, Department of Health and Social Security, August 1971, HMSO.

Pusic, E., Report to the Secretary General of the United Nations on a reappraisal in 1965 of the United Nations Social Service Program (E/CN5/AC12/L3/Add. 1).

Radcliffe-Brown, A. R., *Structure and Function in Primitive Society*, Cohen & West, London, 1952.

Ratcliffe, A. R. and Round, A. E. G., *Transactions of the 17th International Congress of Actuaries*, Vol. III.

Reich, C., *The Greening of America*, Allen Lane, London, 1971; Penguin, Harmondsworth, 1972.

Rein, M., *Social Policy: issues of choice and change*, Random House, New York, 1970.

Report from the House of Commons Expenditure Committee (Education and Arts Sub-Committee), House of Commons Paper 545, 1971.

Report on the Organization and Administration of the Social Services,

Report to United Nations Secretary General by Group of Experts, (ST/SOA/44 and E/CN.5/360/Rev.1), 1962.

Robinson, J., *Economic Philosophy*, Watts, London, 1962.

Royal Commission on Taxation of Income and Profits (Final Report) Cmnd. 9474, HMSO.

Runciman, W. G., *Relative Deprivation and Social Justice*, Routledge & Kegan Paul, London, 1966.

Ruskin, J., *Sesame and Lilies, The Two Paths and King of the Golden River*, Dent, Everyman's Library, London, 1907.

Schorr, A., *Slums and Social Insecurity*, Nelson, London, 1964.

Schumpeter, J. A., *Capitalism, Socialism and Democracy*, Allen & Unwin, 1954.

Slack, K. M., *Social Administration and the Citizen*, Michael Joseph, London, 1966.

Social Insurance and Allied Services, Cmnd. 6424, HMSO, 1942.

Somers, H. M. and Somers, A. R., *Doctors, Patients and Health Insurance*, Brookings Institution, Washington, 1961.

Strategy for Pensions, Department of Health and Social Security, Cmnd. 4755, HMSO, 1971.

Supplementary Benefits Handbook, HMSO, London, November 1972.

Titmuss, R. M., *Essays on the 'Welfare State'*, 2nd ed., Allen & Unwin, London, 1963.

Titmuss, R. M., *Income Distribution and Social Change*, Allen & Unwin, London, 1962.

Titmuss, R. M., *Commitment to Welfare*, Allen & Unwin, London, 1968.

Titmuss, R. M., *The Gift Relationship*, Allen & Unwin, London, 1971.

Titmuss, R. M., 'Welfare Rights: law and discretion', *Political Quarterly*, April 1971.

Titmuss, R. M., 'Social Security and the Six', *New Society*, 11 November 1971.

Transactions of the Faculty of Actuaries, No. 222, 1965.

Veblen, T., *The Theory of the Leisure Class*, Allen & Unwin, London, 1925.

Walley, Sir John, *Social Security, Another British Failure?* Charles Knight, London, 1972.

Wiles, P. J. D. and Markowski, S., 'Income Distribution under Communism and Capitalism', *Soviet Studies*, Nos 3 and 4, 1971.

Wilson, A. T. and Levy, H., *Workman's Compensation*, Oxford University Press, London, 1939.

Wootton, B., *The Social Foundations of Wage Policy*, Allen & Unwin, London, 1955.

INDEX